MARIO BOTTA

MARIO BOTTA

Alessandra Coppa

Motta

Mario Botta

Cover
Church and Pastoral Center Giovanni XXIII, Seriate
Photo
Enrico Cano, Como

Translation
Clarice Zdanski

minimum
essential architecture library

Series edited by Giovanni Leoni

Published Titles

Santiago Calatrava
Richard Meier
Rafael Moneo
Pier Luigi Nervi
Jean Nouvel
Renzo Piano
Álvaro Siza

For the excerpts reproduced in the sections
"Thought" and "Critique," the authors and publishers
wish to thank those who have authorised their
publication. The publisher is available for any queries
regarding sections for which it has not been possible
to trace the holder of the rights.

First Italian Edition: January 2007
First Italian Revised Edition: October 2009
First English Edition: October 2009

ISBN: 978-88-6413-011-8

Printed in Italy

Contents

Portfolio

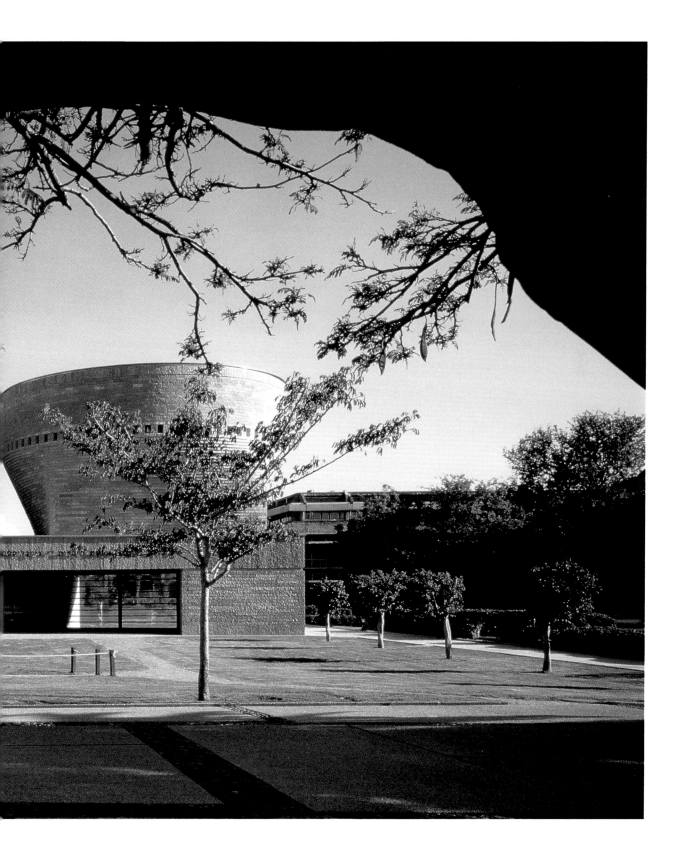

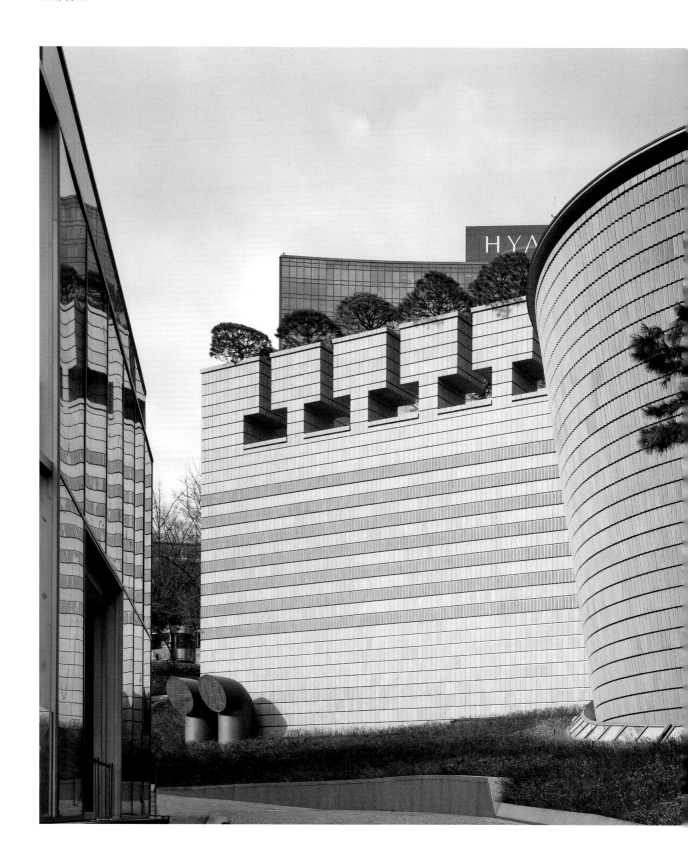

Introduction

Mario Botta, Memory in the Wall

The Method

Since 1963, the year he carried out his first work of architecture (the parish house in Genestrerio), Mario Botta has designed over 300 buildings and works of design, hence an average of eight projects per year, often on a grand scale.

In the course of his long activity designing projects, Mario Botta has constructed and experimented with every type of building: he has expressed great forms and brought little ones to life.

He has not hesitated to raise his investigation into the nature of the symbolic to the heights of a cathedral, to become a mystic in a chapel, or to search for mutual play between art and space in a museum, to give form to a service station or to confront a big office building, to create shelters and private dwellings, or to express the public, in designing stage sets, a chair, a table or a wristwatch.

But there is, nevertheless, a special predilection for the theme of the "home".

In the first years of his career, and through a series of houses, he found out how to develop his own architectural idiom, his own personal style.

"The house is the number one theme for the architect. It embraces the idea of habitat and domesticity and as a consequence, the organization of the space in which man lives: it embraces the idea of a rapport in a context and with the existing territory, and it embraces the memory of the primitive house, the shelter that satisfies one of man's fundamental needs", says Mario Botta[1].

Mario Botta's intense career designing projects is connoted, however, by a precise method that links his personal research to history and to memory with a powerful passion for the profession.

"Botta's method continues to produce according to secure and sophisticated procedures that can be summed up in the idea of memory and in the relationship it has with history [...] visual memory, an inexhaustible source of reference.

The will to see how oneself stacks up against history, to then take it over and make it part of the project itself, and consequence of the visual accumulation that time organizes and criticizes"[2].

A Modern Vitruvius

Mario Botta's architecture brings attention to and seems to rediscover the Vitruvian categories, making them current. Despite a crisis point with the modern movement, Vitruvius' treatise transformed from a historical "text" into a "canon" through the famous triad *utilitas*, *firmitas* and *venustas* (utility, when the distribution of the internal space of each building – whatever its type – is correct and practical to use; solidity, when the foundations, constructed with materials that are carefully chosen without skimping, rest deeply and stably on the underlying soil; beauty, when the aspect of the work is pleasant because of the harmonious proportions of the parts obtained through proper calculation of the symmetries) has never ceased to disturb the ethical and aesthetical imagination of architects since the threshold of modernity.

Elevated to the ranks of meta-historical principle of stabilization, "Vitruvianism" as an attempt to root architecture in its foundations certainly no longer has anything of the original erudite dispute: extending its theoretical ramifications down to the drawing board of architectural practice, it has, as Fulvio Irace[3] has pointed out, become an operative critic and spurs on the re-launching of a constructional ideal that refuses to surrender to the flow of events, only to try to condition and "design" destiny instead. As such it re-emerges, for example, in the theory of "tectonics" as a celebration of the constructional virtues of architecture, as a valorisation of its "material" against its devaluation proposed with insistence by the results of mediatic computerization and the diffusion of the culture of the "immaterial".

Botta writes: "Contemporary architectural culture, through experimentation, lines of current trends or cultural fashions, seems to move away from a confrontation with these primary aspects of construction (light and gravity), almost as if the work of architecture could forego them. In fact, one has the impression that today, operators have other concerns that are no longer directed towards the work constructed, but rather turned towards virtual aspects and comparisons, to ephemeral times, to skin-deep components, to playful aspects,

[1] M. Botta in an interview with G. Cappellato, cit. in *Mario Botta. Poetica dell'architettura*, RCS Libri, Milan 2000.
[2] G. Gresleri, "Bottiana", in *Mario Botta. Luce e Gravità*, 1993-2003, Editrice Compositori, Bologna 2003, p. 14.
[3] F. Irace, "Dimenticare Vitruvio", in *Il Sole 24 Ore*, 16 ottobre 1994, pp. XI-XII.

Sketch for the Dürrenmatt
Centre, Neuchâtel

This architect from Ticino has assimilated Kahn's ratings, and, through his architecture, the classicism of the classical *koinè* and of Hadrian, as well as the teachings of the masters Le Corbusier and Scarpa, who long tormented him, now reach their full maturity. Cataloguer and collector of images, Botta can subject history to an analysis that in any event allows its retrieval, hence making it possible to operate by charging the project with recognizable meanings.

Different repetition

In the lexicon of Mario Botta's architecture, a sort of abacus is found. The compositional rules of this grammar are listed by Pierluigi Nicolin and Mirko Zardini. Many figures recur: the wall and the breach in the wall as fission (understood as a-tectonic element) of "massive" materials like stone and brick, different "holes" and arches that construct the wall and slits with abstract figures; decoration in horizontal courses; vertical inserts of zenithal light; the use of the segmental arch, the arch with interrupted curvature, curvature reproposed in the plan, too; elements of architecture that "break away" towards the landscape, at times like "eyes". Themes like the primary solid and the wall return, the eminence of the façade, light coming from above, the point of reference, the site. Botta's architecture is based on the meaning that he knows how to give to the fundamental values that are immediately recognisable and recurrent in his architectural tales: light, first of all (often from above, sought after and guided inside the volumes); the "detached" or autonomous wall (which enables the construction to present itself as a "boundary" in the landscape); openings (in the manner of Le Corbusier or Kahn) used to select the landscape; the reduction to the essential of walls and internal dividers (so that the space runs fluid and creates continuous connections between distinct parts of building); recessed entrances in the Roman tradition, where the door can be intuited and often is not visible. In fact, Francesco Dal Co speaks of his projects as "places of concentration", where it is possible to re-trace figures belonging to other projects and extrapolate them from the original context. An operation that Botta nevertheless confronts not with narcissism, but rather with the "dialectical consciousness of different repetition" recalled by Gubler[6].

the only ones, it seems, who can still catalyse the interest in debate on the subject"[4].
Among the abovementioned Vitruvian canons, the one that best characterizes Botta's work is *firmitas,* besides geometry, which plays the role of interpreting the reading of space, the angles emphasized and the symmetric order of the walls and of the subtractions.
In Botta's buildings, there is a clear will to retrieve the pleasure produced by the obviousness of the depth and thickness of a curtain wall. In these cases, the wall is transformed from a static technical element into a spatial entity: the openings acquire depth and model the light. The wall of Mario Botta is not an ephemeral event; it has a duration, another category dear to Vitruvius. The material plays a role of primary importance – it gives the wall its own texture and bears witness to its solidity. The facing – in brick or stone – covers the wall in its entirety. The protrusions and recesses of the layers of bricks and the alternations of strips of different coloured stone create shadows and illumination, accentuating the solid presence.
Botta, in short, gives the wall back all of it fullness. The constructed once again becomes a mass, as it was in ancient architecture: it has a body again. This return to building and tectonic tradition paradoxically represents a new route for architecture. The façade ceases to be a tenuous wrapping.
In this sense, Botta's architecture is profoundly "classical". His architecture explores "the archaic of the new"[5], standing "between modern heredity and classical temptation", to the point of excluding, in the latest works, any sort of citation or reference.

[4] G. Cappellato (ed.), *Mario Botta. Luce e Gravità. Architetture 1993-2003*, Editrice Compositori, Bologna 2003, pp. 10-11.
[5] G. Gubler, "Cantieri", in *Mario Botta, Opere complete*, 2, 1985-1990, ed. E. Pizzi, Federico Motta Editore, Milan 1994, p. 7.
[6] Ivi, pp. 6-7.

Thus, Botta's architecture forces us to engage in a patient exercise of attention to the signs used and their metamorphoses. The expedients, studied for a definite solution, can be identified and recognized elsewhere, even if in our recognizing them, they reveal a new statute and new meaning.
Works like the church in Mogno (1986-1996), MART in Rovereto (1988-2002), the Synagogue in Tel Aviv (1996-1998) and the project for the Dürrenmatt Centre in Neuchâtel (1992-2000) contain the profound sense of two twenty-year periods of work. Where themes on which he organized his way of designing projects are experimented with, they are heightened further, purified to the essential, to metaphor, to conceptuality: wall, place, light, volume, now also inter-agents with advanced technology, as in the library in Dortmund (1995-1999), without forgetting the concept of weight and duration.

Sketch for the house in Ligornetto, Switzerland

The Wall

The Image and function of the wall are the primary components of Botta's architecture.
With his inclination towards the solid and the massive, the works of this architect from Ticino intend to express an idea of form and protection that the wall materializes in ways of living, thus acquiring moral meanings and symbolic values.
The tendency to give greater and greater thickness to the wall corresponds to the desire to underline – also formally – the separation between interior and exterior. This tendency to highlight the difference shuns the usual instruments: Botta, in fact, utilizes solid walls, ignoring, unlike much of contemporary architecture, glass and transparency (with the exception of the Bus shelter in Lugano 2000-2001 in polycarbonate, and one of the two volumes of the library in Dortmund), which in any event entail the use of special sources of energy to ensure the comfort of the interior environments. According to an image that Botta loves to repeat, the house cannot be conceived as a "big sick person" fed by conduits, but must find its own physical reality to set against the exterior environment.
In Botta's works, one can note a search for and experimentation on materials that in the course of the years has become more and more precise and attentive, and of which it is possible to follow the evolution. In private residences, for example, the cement brick appears as a constant element, initially

used because economical. A limitation accepted in this way, with time it has come to be a generator of different formal experiments that can enrich solutions studied on each occasion. This use of cement bricks came to be superimposed with chromatic experiments (the homes in Ligornetto 1975-1976 and Massagno 1979), or the play of courses arranged at 45 degrees (homes in Ligrignano 1977-1978), until when the two solutions merged in the house in Morbio Superiore, where the bricks placed at 45 degree angles were coloured silver to produce an accentuated play of chiaroscuro. Above all, research on the use of materials is clear in buildings in which the special configuration of the terrain forced the architect to give preference to a single wall, the wall towards the valley. In these cases, the play of colours and bricks enriches the "façade", thus enabling it to engage in dialogue with the landscape, to represent and describe the face that the house intends to offer. These circumstances, then, demonstrate that Botta does not understand the wall as an expression of closure, but above all as an instrument to project the symbolic values of the building towards the exterior. However, on the other hand, and this is the case with the home in Morbio Superiore, the wall is also the "answer" to the landscape.
If Botta often imagines his buildings to mark off a limit between two environmental or geographical situations, in the same way, his walls – made thicker or reduced to bands of light as in the Banca del Gottardo in Lugano (1982-1988) – represent the threshold to cross before penetrating the interior of the shell of his protected constructions,

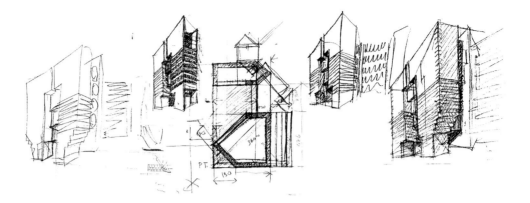

Sketch for the Banca
del Gottardo, Lugano

inside and out, from successions of partitions, arches, screens.

Or Botta works on the "texture" of the wall, as in the case of the Leeum Samsung Museum of Art a Seoul (1995-2004). The architectural language of two simple volumes wedged in between themselves offers a facing in pre-fabricated elements of brick composed of horizontal strips of flat panels for the parallelepiped volume and trapezoidal elements specially designed by Botta for the overturned cone volume.

The place

Instead of "constructing on the site" the building by Botta "constructs the site". When in an open landscape, the building rises to affirm its existence through the solidity of the volume and the geometric order. Emphasizing the vertical dimension or extending along the horizontal axis, its mass is delineated by the geometry of the volume, and its elaborate, disciplined façade relates to the view. When in the city, the façade takes the street elevation into account and responds to this without sacrificing its desire for an independent presence.

Botta's architecture needs the city and its landscape as a dialectic fact, a horizon against which to measure itself. It weaves a critical discourse with the existing: it intends to make itself be accepted as it appears, without merging into or reconciling itself with the site, but rather using it as material in evolution.

The effort that is made in that way is aimed at re-affirming that the vocation of architecture is to go back to comparing itself with its territory, with the

"natural" and with the urban context. Already in the house at Riva San Vitale (1971-73), with a plan that measures 10 metres per side, its presence modified the perception of a characteristic passage of the Ticinese landscape. The little tower that contrasts – so different from the natural elements, from the lay of the land, from the lake surfaces – establishes a sort of ideal boundary to the expansion of the nearby village, and puts itself forward in counterpoint with respect to the church that rises halfway up the hill on the opposite shore of the lake of Lugano.

The new intervention is thus posed as a watershed between parts that assume distinct meanings, as does the school building in Morbio (1972-1977), too. Another opportunity for comparison and dialectic contrast can be seen in the reconstruction of the 30-metre high sectioned model of San Carlo alle Quattro Fontane (1998-2003), in water, executed in Lugano on the occasion of the celebrations marking the date of Borromini's birth.

In the urban interventions, in those that are measured with existent buildings or with the fabric of the city like the bank in Freiburg (1978-1982) or the Rasila 1 building in Lugano (1980-1985) with its moulded corner, here we find the same compositional principle again: the goal in this case is not to signify the "natural" environment, but to capture the differences and the intrinsic meanings of the parts that compose the city.

On the other hand, the perfect insertion of the MART building in Rovereto (1988-2002) in the context comes about with interpretative and monumental naturalness at the same time. The building insists on a site set back with respect to the curtain formed by two period buildings, creating a walkway and a square covered with a glass cupola that becomes the heart of the new installation.

Above and beyond the technical and functional response, Botta also wants the project to be, when necessary, an instrument for a critical re-designing of sectors that, in most cases, have lost their identity – as happened in the Spina Tre neighbourhood in Turin, where Botta had barely completed the parish complex of the church of the Santo Volto (2001-2006), a highly plastic sign, a presence, a generating urban pole that is not indifferent to the fabric of the surroundings.

Light

In Mario Botta's architecture, as the external wrapping is modelled by the play of light on hollow bodies or on surfaces, so, too is the internal volume defined and animated by the presence of light. Thus the effects of light inside the building correspond to the play of the plastic forms of the external walls. Rejecting the succession of windows, Botta is led to articulate the functions performed by traditional openings through different architectural solutions, which are configured as spaces of mediation, or as little openings in the walls. Above all, however, they are resolved in the privilege granted to the zenithal source of light, which is given the task of illuminating and giving life both to the most hidden as well as the most important parts of the building. Botta entrusts the different sources of light with the task of differentiating space and, both in private as well as public buildings , the zenithal light in particular is given the task of indicating the presence of the most important elements, the skeleton on which the building is organized.
In Botta's architecture, then, the skylight is only the most evident signal of research designed to configure a precise internal hierarchy of spaces and to give them a prevalently vertical organization. The light, which descends from above in the heart of the building, underlines, on the other hand, introversion and the desire to turn inside rather than outside, a characteristic of many of Botta's works. This is demonstrated by projects like the foyer of the theatre in Chambery (1982), surrounded by a ring of zenithal light, and the library in Villeurbanne (1984), which lives because of the great central empty space along which the pathways that the main spaces look out onto unwind.
In sacred architecture, the use of light constructs the space, enriching it with symbolic meaning. This happens starting with the church of San Giovanni

Battista in Mogno, where the oblique, glass surface of the covering orients the building in relation to the sun, and continuing until the more recent church in Seriate (1994/2000-2004), where the space is characterised by the light caught by the horizontal panels covered with very thin gold leafing that captures the natural light and by two small, light apses that, barely hinted at, break through the limit of the church and make whoever enters perceive the light from above that dramatically strikes the bas-relief by Giuliano Vangi.

Volume

In Mario Botta's architecture, volume is defined *a priori*. It is not the result of the aggregation of different parts. Nor is it a product or final derivation. It is designed and defined from the beginning. The building needs to have an identity that can be read. The aspect of its volume performs this function; it makes the building a representation of an autonomous object situated in the landscape, immobile and self-sufficient. But the building is not indifferent to what is around it; it engages in dialogue with the environment, affirming its own presence.
Volume presents a primary form that is not distorted or deformed. It can be transformed, but its origin is always clear: the square or the triangle, the rectangle or the cylinder, although with multiple variations.
It does not necessarily have to be a single volume. Generally, we find a principal volume that gives form to everything. Minor volumes are distinct from the main one; the parallelepiped is distinct from the cylinder, as is the straight line from the curved line. When there are more volumes, their conjunction follows precise rules. Botta uses the axes of symmetry.
The power of the message will not be undermined by asymmetrical variations. Symmetry will be the main rule of order.
The primary solid does not remain intact: subtractions from its mass create a play on positive and negative spaces; they create spaces of transition, intermediate spaces between the inside and the outside.
Volume is emptied out because what is outside enters to become part of it, to give it shelter from the outside and draw it closer to the inside.
The cylinder occupies a special place in his choice

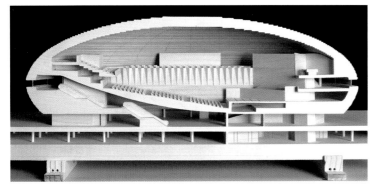

Above
Cutaway model, Teatro alla Scala, Milan

Below
Cutaway model of the new auditorium, Rimini

creates a powerful atrium for the Harting office building in Minden (1999-2001). Then again, reduced to pure containing wall, it shapes a gallery space for the Friedrich Dürrenmatt Centre in Neuchâtel. Instead, on a hill above the ample vineyard in Suvereto, in the hinterland around Piombino, the Petra vineyards (1999-2003) presents itself through the image of a cylinder in Prun stone, sectioned with a diagonal plan parallel to the hill and two colonnaded building bodies on the sides and oriented towards the sea.

There is also an elliptical plan in the recent project for the new auditorium in Rimini, which is configured as archi-sculpture. Nevertheless, the building has the primary form of a shell raised with respect to the ground floor. A single horizontal fissure at the centre brings together and separates the two shells in the hall of the auditorium below and of the respective covering above.

Openings

Openings are like incisions cut into the primary volume, which thus assumes force because of them. It is above all through the operations of digging into volumes that Botta establishes the connection with the human scale. He avoids treating the problem of the relationship between inside and outside, thus reducing himself to designing traditional surfaces pierced by windows, but at the same time, he shows that he is contrary to the modern idea of encouraging the disappearance of the solid to the benefit of openings.

For example, on the outside of Botta's houses, there are neither windows, nor doors, nor glass walls; each construction is taken back to essentiality, to its articulations of the relationships between solids and voids.

The buildings are like hollowed out volumes endowed with their own sculptural values. This attitude can already be grasped starting from the first creations, like the houses in Cadenazzo (1970-1971) and Riva San Vitale. Rejecting the congruence between interior and exterior, these two buildings, although so different, interpret the same idea of a "house within a house". Botta immediately perceives the importance of the element of mediation between interior and exterior, and he enriches it to the point of recovering the tradition of porticoes and loggias,

of primary solids; since it can be clearly read and is devoid of ambiguity, it gives a sense of presence to the building. In its different apparitions, it re-affirms its own expressive power.

The symbolism and clarity of the cylindrical form are preferred to represent collective space, whether involving a theatre or a church. In Mogno, for example, the cylinder has a horizontal elliptical section. In his work at the Teatro alla Scala (2000-2002), besides the volume of the stage tower that represents the most important construction of the bodies of the backstage area inscribed in a parallelepiped set back by two and one half metres with respect to the Via Verdi façade, a new volume on a elliptical plan was raised where the numerous services required are located (small dressing rooms, changing rooms, etc.); this "new" volume, added above the roofs, is located on the side of the volume of the stage, and is equipped with its own autonomous image.

The cylinder can also be divided into sections: half of a cylinder defines the turning corner and gives a street façade to the Union de Banques Suisses in Basel (1986-1995). Truncated once more, at the same time cut in half and made elliptical in plan, it putting it forward as an autonomous space that envelops the house proper. A gradual sequence of thresholds and passages that can create pathways through the volumes substitutes the immediacy of the transition between interior and exterior. Instead, what Botta seems to follow is a sort of reversal of transparency, taking it back to the interior of the building. In fact, the loggias of the house in Massagno (1979) and Viganello (1980) appear as reversed bow-windows, projecting towards the inside rather than the outside: the house seems to want to look inside itself.

Thus Botta's architecture presupposes extremely precise designing of the relationship towards the outside, which, rather than becoming concrete in openings that are indifferent to the landscape, is expressed in selective closures of certain parts, rejecting the panorama, to privilege a view.

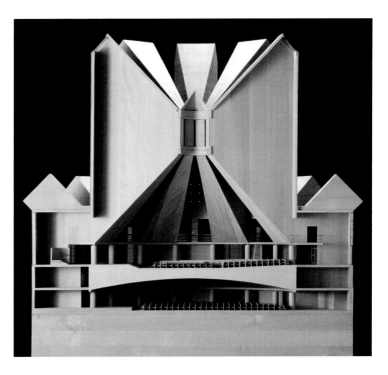

Cutaway model of the church of the Santo Volto, Turin

Sacred Space

For Mario Botta, to construct a church today means confrontation with some questions with respect to the role and meanings that the work of architecture must assume in the urban context. His churches with annexed parvises in Pordenone (1987-1992), in Sartirana (1987-1995) and in Seriate, the cathedral of Evry and the evocative façade of the parish church in Genestrerio (1959-1963) in Ticino represent answers aimed at these clearly understood questions.

However, for Botta, the church in the revived village of Mogno is "the architectural place" like no other. Here it is possible to decipher meanings present in the sacred works constructed thereafter. Light reigns sovereign; it pours in, flows, defines, to the point of making the stone that the volume is made of light and "transparent", and the stone volume, with its ellipsoidal plan, finds its solar disc as it rises. "From the philosophical and theological point of view, it is a parallel of the rectangular space controlled by the terrestrial ellipse and the circular roof of the sacred kingdom"[7].

When he was hired to find a solution for the Cymbalista Synagogue in Tel Aviv, in a diverse urban situation that was not very compact, Botta again put forward the theme of the square and the circle, here connected one inside the other. Through formidable tapering of the bands of masonry facing that rise, the polygon of the base and that of the roof are superimposed as in a mirror, while around

them the walls pass progressively from the cubic figure to the cylindrical one. The resulting void between inscribed square and circumscribed circle serves to make zenithal light go down into the inside, varying with the variation of the sun's course and reaching the earth refracted by the harshness and vibrancy of the inner surfaces. Botta reassumes and secularises, in this case, a theme that he had taken on at Mogno and in the powerful bulwark of the chapel on Monte Tamaro (1990-1995) with pathos never seen before. Never as on these occasions have these building-places *par excellence* served to create another place, precisely where there was none. In a highly destructured world, the sacred building can thus be understood (apart from the practice and religious function that belong to it) not only as a sign of being Christian or Hebrew or Muslim, but as something that represents man in his complexity and the world itself in its sacredness. In this sense, Botta has also defined the museum as "the new modern cathedral", so much so that the museum in San Francisco (1989-1995) could be compared to the cathedral of Evry (1988-1995). But there is more, underlines Mario Botta: "The interesting aspect of this approach is that through the investigation of sacred spaces, I discovered the themes and principles that motivate architecture itself"[8], or the idea of the enclosure, the threshold, the wall.

[7] R. Arnheim, "Note a proposito dell'architettura religiosa", in *Domus*, 757, 1994, pp. 82-85.
[8] M. Botta, "Costruire una chiesa", in *Chiesa a Seriate*, Skira, Milan 2004, p. 23.

Chronology

1943	Born in Mendrisio, Switzerland
1959	Carried out his first work: the parish house in Genestrerio, in consultation with Tita Carloni, in whose studio he worked as building designer/draughtsman Single-family home, Morbio Superiore
1964	Began studies at the Istituto Universitario di Architettura in Venice (IUAV)
1965	Worked at Le Corbusier's Studio in Venice
1969	Met and collaborated with Louis I. Kahn in Venice. Took his degree in architecture with Carlo Scarpa and Giuseppe Mazzariol as readers Beginning of independent professional activity with a studio in Lugano
1970	Single-family home, Cadenazzo
1972	Middle School, Morbio Inferiore
1973	Biblioteca dei Cappuccini, Lugano
1975	Single-family home, Ligornetto; house, Manno, Switzerland
1976	Invited as Professor at the Ecole Polytechnique Fédérale (EPFL) in Lausanne
1977	Municipal gymnasium and crafts centre, Balerna Transformation of a farm, Ligrignano, Morbio Inferiore
1978	Banca dello Stato, Freiburg, Switzerland
1979	Single-family homes, Pregassona and Massagno, Switzerland Competition project for urban reconstruction in Basel Project for terraced houses, Riva San Vitale
1980	Single-family homes, Viganello and Stabio, Switzerland Ransila 1 administrative building, Lugano House, Origlio
1982	Member of the Swiss Federal Fine Arts Commission, position held until 1987 Maison de la Culture André Malraux, Chambery Single-family home, Morbio Superiore, Switzerland Banca del Gottardo, Lugano Began to create a series of design objects, like chairs, lamps and clocks
1983	Regular Professor, Ecole Polytechnique Fédérale (EPFL) in Lausanne Honorary member, BDA-Bund Deutscher Architekten
1984	Honorary member, AIA- American Institute of Architects Library, Villeurbanne, France Exhibit "Carlo Scarpa 1906-1978", Gallerie dell'Accademia, Venice Ransila 2 administrative building, Lugano
1985	Exhibit space ICF Design Center, New York Watari-Um Art Gallery, Tokyo Office and apartment building, Berlin Residential building and Studio Mario Botta in Via Ciani, Lugano Installation of exhibit "Mario Botta Architetture 1960-1985", Venice, with Achille Castiglioni
1986	Monographic exhibit, Museum of Modern Art, Chicago Architecture Award Remodelling of the new headquarters of the Banca dello Stato in Bellinzona

Church of San Giovanni Battista, Mogno, Valle Maggia
New headquarters of the Union de Banques Suisses, Basel
Residential and commercial building Centro Cinque Continenti, Lugano-Paradiso
Caimato administrative building, Lugano Cassarate
First project for the Piazza della Pace, Parma

1987 Invited as Professor at the Yale School of Architecture New Haven, Connecticut
Church of Beato Odorico, Pordenone
Exhibit "Une architecture-trois habitats", Ecole des arts décoratifs, Geneva
New church of San Pietro Apostolo, Sartirana di Merate, with Fabiano Redaelli
Banque Bruxelles Lambert, Geneva

1988 Received the title *Chevalier* in the Ordre des Arts et des Lettres, Paris
Cathedral of the Resurrection, Evry
Museo d'arte moderna e contemporanea, Rovereto, with Giulio Andreolli

1989 *Laurea Honoris Causa* at the Escuela de Altos Estudios del CAYC, Buenos Aires and awarded the prize CICA – International Committee of Architectural Critics, International Biennial of Architecture, Buenos Aires
Museum of Modern Art, San Francisco, California, with Hellmuth, Obata & Kassabaum

1989 Kyobo Tower, Seoul

1990 Chapel of Santa Maria degli Angeli, Monte Tamaro, Switzerland
New Casinò, Campione d'Italia

1991 Honorary member, Académie d'Architecture de France, Paris
Exhibit "Mario Botta Architectures 1980-1990", Musée Rath, Geneva
Ten single-family homes, Bernareggio

1992 Centre Dürrenmatt, Neuchâtel, Switzerland
Museum Jean Tinguely, Basel

1993 Honorary member, Accademia di belle arti di Brera, Milan
Liceo Scientifico, Città della Pieve

1994 Honorary member, CAM-SAM, Colegio de Arquitectos de la Ciudad de Mexico-Sociedad de Arquitectos Mexicanos, Mexico City
Housing development in the ex-Appiani area, Treviso
Remodelling of the Fondazione Querini Stampalia, Venice
Church of Giovanni XXIII and pastoral centre, Paderno-Seriate

1995 European Prize for Culture, Karlsruhe
Biblioteca Tiraboschi, Bergamo
Noah's Ark, open-air museum of Niki de Saint Phalle's sculpture, Jerusalem
Municipal library, Dortmund
Leeum - Samsung Museum of Art, Seoul

1996 Under the auspices of the constitution of the Università della Svizzera Italiana, drew up the programme for the institution for an academy of architecture in Mendrisio; since October 1996 engaged in teaching there
Honorary member, Accademia svizzera delle scienze tecniche
Awarded the Merit Award for Excellence in Design-AIA, California, for the San Francisco Museum of Modern Art
Cymbalista Synagogue and Jewish Heritage Centre, Tel Aviv, with Arthur Zylberzac
Tata Consultancy Services administrative building, New Delhi

1997 Awarded Honorary Fellowship, RIBA, London
Awarded the Marble Architectural Award America, Carrara, for the San Francisco Museum of Modern Art
Exhibit "Emozioni di pietra", Palazzo Reale, Naples

1998 Professional training tower, Moron, the Jura, Switzerland

	Wooden model for the church of San Carlo alle Quattro Fontane for the exhibit on Borromini, Lugano Exhibit "Licht und Materie", Deutsches Architekturzentrum, Berlin
1999	*Chevalier* in the Ordre national de la Legion d'Honneur, Paris Marble Architectural Award Europe, for the church of San Giovanni Battista in Mogno, Switzerland Cantina Petra, Suvereto Project for the University of Trento Office district, Tata Consultancy Services, Hyderabad, India
2000	Project for the Bechtler Museum, Charlotte, North Carolina Headquarters of Assicurazione Nazionale in Athens, with Morfo Papanikolau and Irena Sakellaridou Church of the Santo Volto, Turin Project for the chapel in Azzano Remodelling of the Teatro alla Scala, Milan
2002	Requalification and salvaging of the Porto Vecchio, Trieste Marble Architectural Award Middle East, Cymbalista Synagogue and Jewish Heritage Centre, Tel Aviv
2003	Exhibit "Luce e Gravità", Padua Tschuggen Hotel - Berg Oase Arosa, Ticino
2004	Annual Seoul Architectural Award: Grand Award for the Kyobo Tower in Seoul Samsung offices, Seoul New hospital, Vimercate
2005	Decorated as Officer in the Ordine al merito della Repubblica Italiana, Rome Awarded the Premio Grinzane Cavour - Sezione Alba Pompeia, Alba Awarded the IOC/IAKS prize, granted by the International Olympic Committee, Koln, for the National Youth Sports Center in Tenero, Switzerland Exhibit "Architetture del Sacro - Preghiere di Pietra" in Florence and later at the RIBA in London Continuing education campus, Banca BPL Subway, Naples Museo dell'architettura, Mendrisio New office district for the state police, Padua
2006	Professor Dottor Honoris Causa, Faculty of Theology, University of Freiburg, Switzerland Great Mosque, Zarqa, Jordan Parish of San Rocco di Sambuceto, San Giovanni Teatino, Italy
2007	Professor Dottor Honoris Causa, Humanities Department, University of Neuchâtel, Switzerland Design "Guscio", installation Confindustria Ceramica, Milan Competition for Xixi Wetland Museum, Hangzhou, China Installation of the exhibit on Titian. Ultimo atto, Palazzo Crepadona, Belluno Kostantinovsky Conference Centre, St. Petersburg Competition for urban development, Zorlu Centre, Istanbul Competition for the new Swiss embassy in Moscow Competition for the new headquarters of the penal court in Bellinzona, Switzerland Competition for the Johor Iconic Park, Malaysia
2008	Tshingua University Library, Beijing Project for Korean Air Songhyeon-Dong, Seoul Competition "Centro di Pronto Intervento", Mendrisio Competition for European Embankment Project, St. Petersburg

Unless otherwise indicated, the year in which each work was commissioned is indicated

Works

Banca del Gottardo
Lugano, Switzerland, 1982-1988

Sketch of the project

The volumetric composition, which starts from the fractioned organization, becomes the direct expression of the possibility of a new way of city development that is opposed in a precise way to the anonymous processes of tertiary transformation. Great architectural figures characterize the monumental image of the front of the new construction. A succession of high towers are pushed forward to affirm the presence of the new institution in an imperative way, while the rest of the construction recedes to design a landscape of courtyards open towards the city.

The public space is insinuated in the jagged profile of the plan of the building, thus offering the image of a different kind of permeability of the construction and creating multiple occasions for viability that find a natural

conclusion in the system of accesses placed in the shelter of the wing walls against which the bulk of the massive foreparts rests. Each of them leads into great spaces where the different functions of bank take place: tellers' windows, a restaurant, an independent entrance to the offices, an art gallery. Above, the void of a volume that reaches up to the summit of the building, illuminated from above by a triangular glass, innervates the spatial organization of each unit, creating a singular point of reference where the relations between the work spaces converge on the different floors. The system of pathways envelops this volume with triangular balconies, articulating a stellar distribution of the various work spaces that look outside into the penumbra designed by the great sculpted wings of the sunblinds.

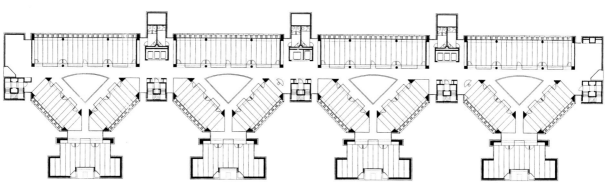

Above
View of the entrance

Below
Plan

Opposite page
Façade of one of the blocks
of the complex

Church of San Giovanni Battista
Mogno-Fusio, Ticino, Switzerland, 1986-1996

The church seen in the context of the Valle Maggia

The basic idea for this project was born of the annihilation caused by an avalanche that destroyed part of the village and the seventeenth century church in 1986. The reflection concentrates on the relationship between the construction, as expression of man's daily toil and his presence in the territory, and the boundless force of nature that characterizes the approach to the project. The thick wall mass of stone at the base, which characterizes the entire plan, is skilfully lightened by the progressive tapering of the courses up to the lightness evoked by the glass covering.

The interior plan is obtained by a rectangle inscribed in an ellipse, which is transformed

into a circle in correspondence to the roof. The space of the church is oriented according to the guiding line of the minor axis of the ellipse that becomes a circle at the level of the covering appropriately inclined. The ellipse, a symbol of the anxiety of the human condition, thus contrasts with the prefect circular form in the sky. The powerful structure of the two flying buttresses, which connect the wall facing the valley to the one facing the mountain, emphasizes the character of resistance required of the architecture. Through alternating bands in two colours, the building system highlights the stratification typical of construction in stone and enphasizes the weight of the work through this technique.

Mart - Museo d'arte moderna e contemporanea
Rovereto, Italy, 1988-2002

Plan

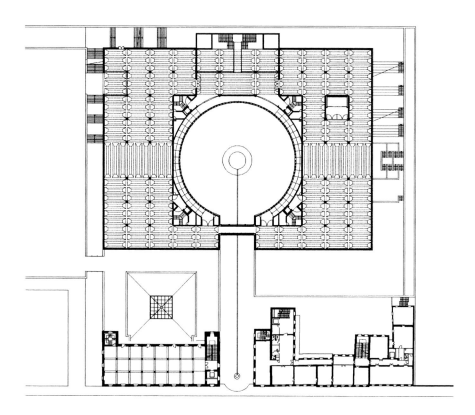

The new museum in Rovereto is in Corso Bettini where the Palazzo Alberti and the Palazzo del Grano are located. An axial composition, the project is organized along the lane between the two buildings, and the lane is prolonged inside, so that it becomes a central square around which all of the activities required by the programme are structured. This composition makes it possible to preserve the character of the lane with its period buildings, and to enhance these same buildings through new structures in the rear part. The part in expansion has the characteristics of a building on three floors above ground organized around a central courtyard that is recalled perspectivally along Corso Bettini. A vast green area faces, to the north, the construction of the new media library through the formation of a park behind the former Maffei theatre. This space is both a

Entrance to the square
covered by a skylight

reference and empty counterpoint to the powerful building and fabric constructed by the Centre. The main entrance corresponds to the entrance façade of the circular plaza, while two other sectors with independent entrances branch off from the central courtyard. One leads to the space of the auditorium-philharmonic hall; the other, to the library, physically connected to the Palazzo del Grano. This sector is organized with a ground floor and a sunken storey so as to be able to respond to plans to enlarge the present municipal library and historical archive. The service and administration areas of the museum are situated on the first level of the two period buildings. The new museum exhibit spaces are in the new construction. The central square, covered with a glass cupola, also offers the visitor a place where different activities can be held in the open air.

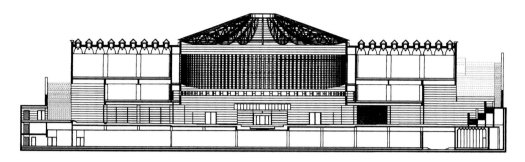

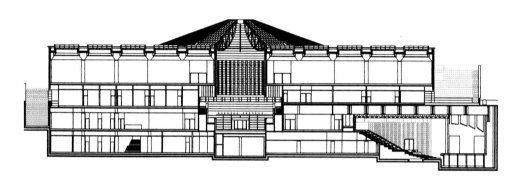

Cross and longitudinal sections

Opposite page
Above
View from above of the central monumental staircase

Below
Exhibit space

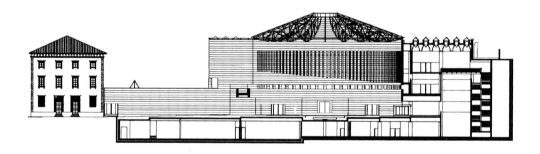

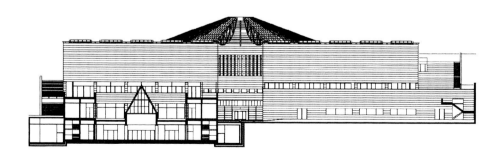

Moma - Museum of Modern Art
San Francisco, Usa, 1989-1995

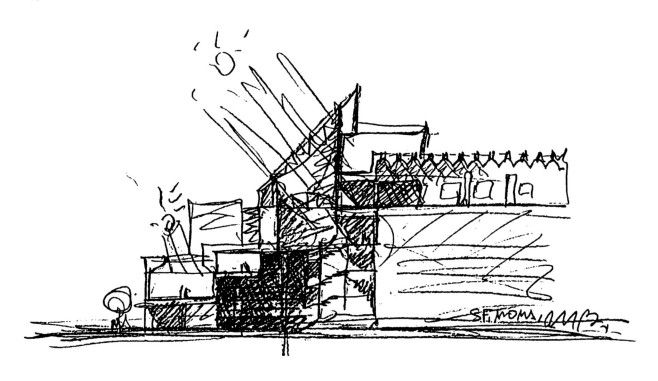

Study sketch

The project expresses the simplicity together with the complexity of an architectural gesture that can define an autonomous presence in the city and construct a point of reference at the same time. Locating the building on a lot bordering on three high buildings suggested the choice of a particularly strong image that nevertheless escapes a direct confrontation with the emerging structures around it. The work has three objectives. In the first place,

there is natural light, with its ability to create a close relationship with the site, with its colours, with its luminosity and with the possibility of offering a different reading from the works on display. Hence there is an idea of the construction of a centre of encounter and collective confrontation on the great themes of culture, where nevertheless the values of memory are present and the sensitivity of other men with respect to history is born witness to.

The whole of the internal pathways has been shaped so as to maintain a constant rapport with the vast central space that runs through the construction vertically, giving an immediate reading to the functional organization of the different spaces. Finally, there is the need to measure itself against the site and the city, in a rapport aimed at bringing the city inside the museum and sending out its values and meaning for the community. The necessity was

thus to oppose the indiscriminate use of iron and glass with the reality of ancient materials like brick and stone, which can communicate the diversity of the construction, and to extend into what has been defined as a sort of "innovative upheaval", in which forms and volumes constantly lend themselves to a twofold reading with no ambiguity whatsoever, almost as if to identify spaces arranged in them as an inseparable part of the city.

Placement of the museum in the urban context

Page 48
Above
Suspended walkway
Below
Plan of the levels

Page 49
Exhibit space with natural lighting

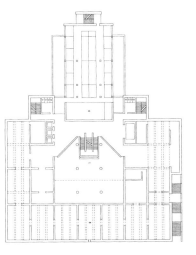
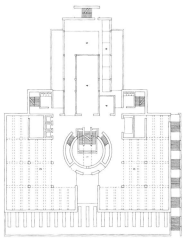
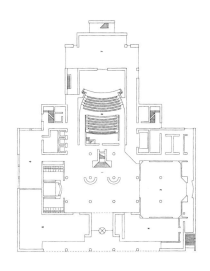

Kyobo Tower
Seoul, South Korea, 1989-2003

Placement of the tower in
the urban context

The new building of the Kyobo insurance
company in Seocho is located at an
important road junction that relates the
different urban parts.
The location of this site suggests a powerful
image as a point of reference in the complex
city fabric. The exceptional nature of this
work consists in the play on the contrast
between the great full volumes and the
empty cuts that alternate different scales of

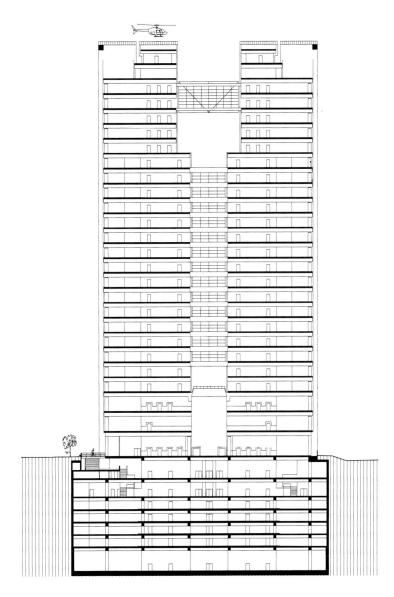

reading, from the depth of the landscape to the refined details of the masonry in terracotta. Its vertical image, powerful and strong, sets it apart as a contemporary fortress that can attract attention as a new urban sign, a recognizable presence beyond the functional contents (offices) that characterize it.

On the side of the main relief road, the upper floors of the building have two distinct blocks connected by a narrow glassed-in passage that unites the vertical units.

The outer bodies are massive thanks to the rhythm of the *brise-soleil* outer protection, while in the centre, the building has a fragile skin. A transparent heart characterizes the core of the tower, which offers a new landscape – a great constructed garden with access on different levels.

The part of the building on the tops of the towers, however, has a lens-shaped roof that protects the ample terraces of the top floors.

Above
Section

Below
Plan

View of the tower

Opposite page
View of the entrance hall

Chapel of Santa Maria degli Angeli
Monte Tamaro, Switzerland, 1990-1996

View of the body of the
church from the soffit
of the aerial connection

The construction "breaks away" from the mountain, tracing out a horizon and taking the form of a chapel in the lower part, the head of an ideal viaduct.

The whole is a manipulation of the existing landscape: the plastic forms, the transversal incisions, the new geometric configurations – all are modelled "in the negative" below the line of the horizon traced out by the communication trench. Inside, the space of the church is structured in three aisles, of which the central, lower one is marked at the entrance by two powerful columns. It converges in the space of the little end apse that protrudes from the primary volume. Intense zenithal light inundates this little apse, insisting on the sign of prayer in the two hands on the walls, a work by Enzo Cucchi. The inner perimeter of the chapel is marked by twenty-two openings at the floor level, which make it possible to discover the extraordinary landscape of the valley. They also hold, in the splay of the wall, a series of paintings on the theme of Our Lady of the Angels. The inner space lives on the great contrast between the circular black slaked lime walls without form and the linear white mouldings of the ceiling, which let in a "moustache" of light cut out from the steps of the covering.

Axonometry of the complex

Above
Side elevation

Below
View of the apse with
the works of Enzo Cucchi

Opposite page
The church in the valley
of Tamaro in the snow

Above
View of the apse next to
the church of St. Alexander

Right
The inside with the bas-
relief by Giuliano Vangi
in the apse

Opposite page
Detail of the covering

Municipal library
Dortmund, Germany, 1995-1999

Axonometry

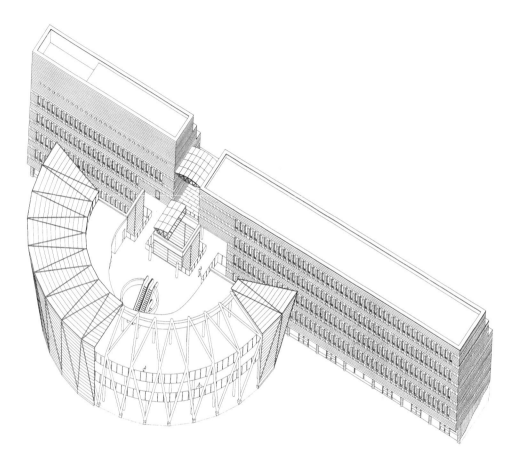

The high stone wall that looks out onto the open area opposite the station defines a new limit of the constructed urban space. The great wing interrupted only by the web of delicate fissures, restores to the façade an image of compactness and solidity.
A cloud of glass emerges from this austere surface and bursts into the green space before it, revealing, in the transparency, the articulation of the inner spaces. A double glass casing enshrouds the structure of steel piers that reach upwards to support the transparent disc of the covering. Inside, the circular joists of the two floors that hold the spaces for reading and consulting books withdraw from the structures of the piers of this wrapping, standing free in all of their height.

Access to the structure is located behind this truncated cone volume at the centre of a protected pathway that separates it from the volume of the linear building. A series of escalators rises along the circular cavity, obtained from the ceiling, thus making it possible to reach the upper floors.
Glass bridges prolong the reading rooms inside the spaces in the rectangular body of the building. A progressive tapering of the body of the edifice on the different floors allows for a series of terraces on the façade that looks out onto the city, and they facilitate the entrance of natural light into the interior environments, while at the same time separating the building from the frontage of existing constructions near the library.

General view of the building

Page 64
Detail of the masonry opposite the glass wall

Page 65
View of the reading room

Cymbalista Synagogue and Jewish Heritage Centre
Campus of the University of Tel Aviv, Israel, 1996-1998

View of the main façade

The project for the synagogue and Jewish heritage centre on the campus at the University of Tel Aviv is a point of reference with respect to other urban components. The special quality of this architecture lies in the fact that it planned for the creation of a building destined for two main activities: a synagogue and a conference room, which form the fundamental elements of the area in question in this project. The two spaces are connoted by two different, specific tasks. The project synthesizes the two functions – a place of prayer and a place of cultural encounter – transforming them into an

architectural image of equal formal value. The construction starts from the base perimeter of the service volumes oriented towards the south and placed on the ground floor, together with a central atrium accessed by two main façades oriented towards the north. The two identical spaces, on a square plan, form a circle at the level of the covering through the progressive widening of the walls as they gradually rise, becoming two similar towers that characterize the whole of the work.

In each volume, four arcs, obtained from the circular perimeter with the square of the roof inscribed in it, are put forward as inlets of light and in this way diffuse luminosity from above, which floods in onto the inner walls and down to the floor. The equivalence of the two volumes is plastic as well as formal and symbolic, and corresponds to a typological choice that expresses the twofold opportunity of creating a space that is religious and at the same time secular.

Above
View of the back of a tower

Right
Cross-section

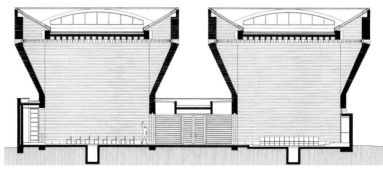

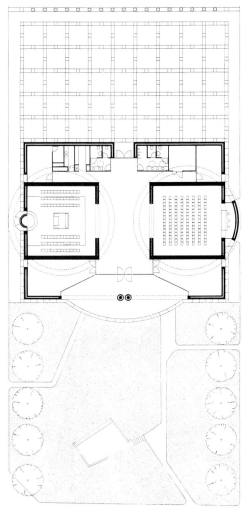

Above
Left
Detail of the covering with
zenithal light
Right
Plan

Opposite left
Entrance

Opposite page
Interior

Church of the Santo Volto
Turin, Italy, 2001-2006

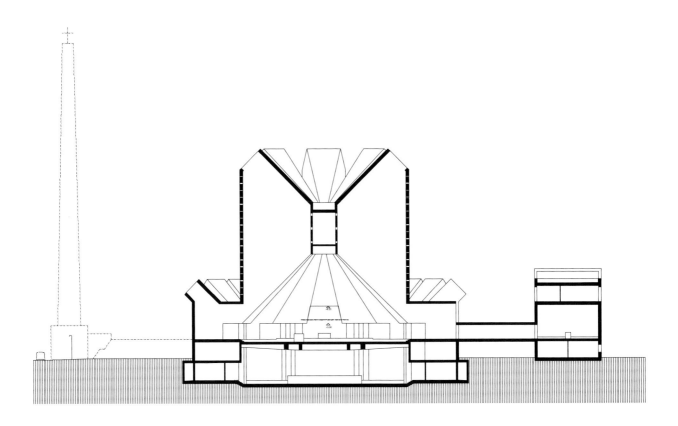

Cross-section

Fruit of a "plan for urban requalification" intended to reintegrate the abandoned industrial areas of the 1970s into the urban fabric, the building offers a new urban quality. The complex includes a church, an underground hall for assemblies and conferences, offices of the metropolitan curia, apartments, a weekday chapel for everyday functions, a presbytery and various structures for education and recreation.

The central plan church is surrounded by seven perimetral towers to which are added the lower bodies of the chapels that, thanks to the truncated upper end, also function as skylights. The heptagonal plan has made it possible to orient the inner hall according to an entrance-altar axis turned towards the city. The pyramidal covering generates the inner void through an alternation of solids and voids that rotate around a central drum. Despite the constructional complexity and vast dimensions, the hall transmits a pleasant, welcoming sensation and makes it possible to establish a subtle relationship

View of the parvis

with the external environment since light, coming from the towers of the chapels, is modulated and changes colour and intensity from partition to partition . Moreover, little glass blocks framed in cement allow a punctuation of light on the vertical walls. Following the requests of those who commissioned the work, the architect and his collaborators reconstructed the face of Jesus impressed on the "holy shroud" through a skilful interweaving of stone worked with two different forms and mounted so as to have a wedge side that would create shadows and a flat side to reflect the light. An integral part of the project is that the smokestack from the former steelworks has been retained, rising as a symbol of work and workers' culture. A spiralling ring in stainless steel with "unciform" arms rises from the parvis to the summit that ends in a cross over sixty metres from the ground. The bells are small, and are mounted at the base of the tower on a rectangular frame corresponding to the main entrance.

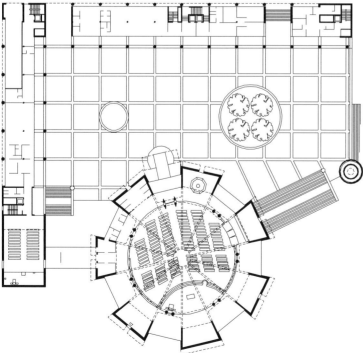

Above
Detail of the covering

Below
Plan of the ground floor

View of the interior from
the entrance

Projects

Municipal Casinò
Campione d'Italia, Italy, 1990-2006

View of the complex from
the lake

Opposite page
Above
General planimetry
Below
Cross-section

The area planned for the new city gambling house and related services is in a position adjacent to the urban concentration of the historical centre and at the foot of the hill that rises above Campione d'Italia. This area is thus a place in which different geographical contexts and building structures live together: on the one hand, the group of historical constructions; on the other, the twentieth century structures. This special quality lies at the base of the layout of the design that traces out two pedestrian areas, from the mountain to the lake, perpendicular to the adjacent structures. The building of the new gambling house is concentrated uphill, and rises up to a maximum height of four floors. The concentration of the constructed volume in the upper part allows the creation of a great urban park below present-day Piazza Milano.

The park constitutes a system of voids in counterpoint to the great overhanging volume and an urban space of convergence of the two adjacent lateral structures.

CASINO MUNICIPALE

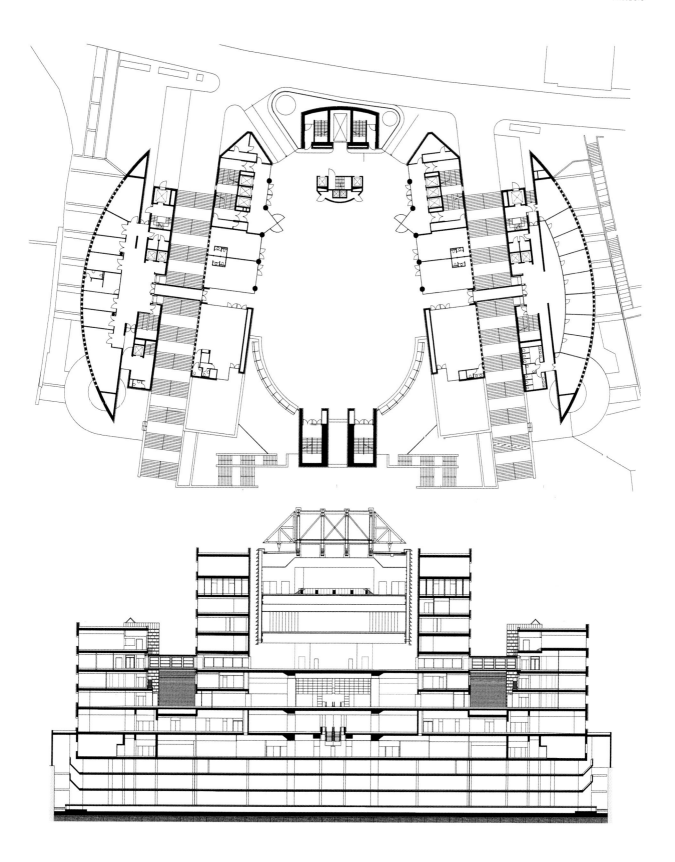

Housing development in the ex-Appiani area
Treviso, Italy, 1994 (in construction)

Aerial view, render

The project calls for a "mending" of the empty urban complex between Viale Monte Grappa and Viale della Repubblica, an area that was once the headquarters of the Appiani ceramics industry. The area is located at about 400 metres from the sixteenth century city walls that delimit the historical centre. The main theme is the design of a square at the centre of buildings used for headquarters of institutions, residential places and business zones, different among themselves in typology and volumetry. The project foresees the formation of an underground parking lot of about 1500 parking places. In the future, the new area will be able to be connected to the roundabout planned so as to facilitate the possibility of a regional link. The job aims for the transformation of the current outskirts from simple residential zones to organisms with their own figurative and functional values, so as to re-evoke the high quality of life evident in the historical city centre, which also owes a great deal to keeping the zones in question green.

Planimetry of the site

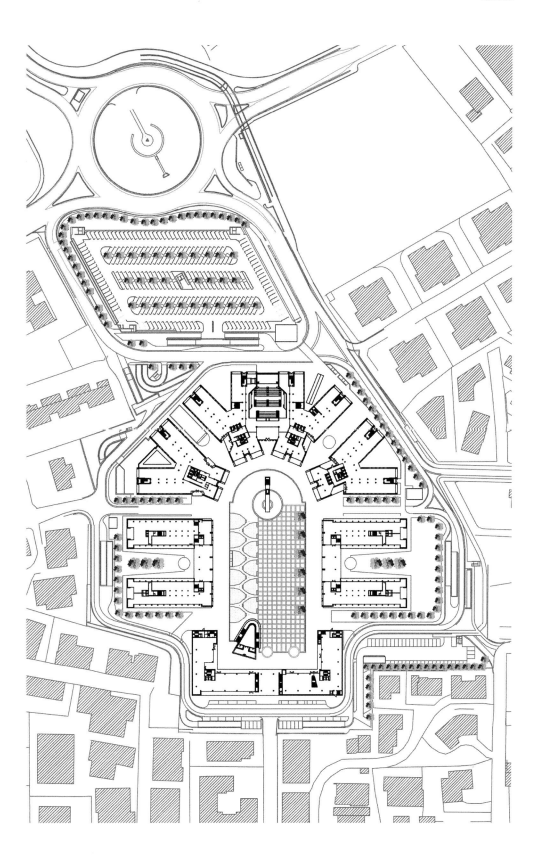

New Central Library
University, Trento, Italy, 1999

Model

Opposite page
Left
Study sketches

Right
From above
Plans and longitudinal
section

The area of San Severino chosen for the location of the new library, the construction of which is planned for 2007-2010, is at the end of Via Verdi near the river, in a position that marks the limits of the city. It is a flat zone that is currently being used as a public parking area with access directly from the Lungo Adige San Severino. Although it is situated beyond the railroad tracks, which for some time distinctly separated the historical city from twentieth century expansion along the river, the area is directly related to the Duomo located at the opposite end of the Via Verdi axis. The project intends to valorise this ideal link by restoring the system of routes of the historical city and closely relating the new library to the whole of decentralized university functions a short distance away. The new building is placed as the last urban element before the caesura of the river. It is assumed as the final element in an ideal link with the city centre, with an even more closed side towards the river and turned towards the direction of the Duomo and other institutions. One suggestion for intervention was to construct a sort of corner open to the city so that it might start a semantic and symbolic dialogue with the new structure. Behind the

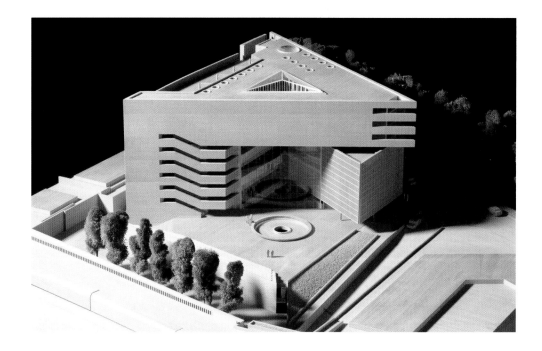

glass façade turned towards the city, it will be possible to take in the central void on which the reading spaces are located vertically, the shelves with the volumes arranged in an orderly way behind so as to make a sort of open box. Moreover, the façade rises on a new public square closely related to the system of pedestrian routes that, through the bicycle and walking path tunnel already existing along Via Verdi and the new underpass beyond the Mulino Vittoria, will be aimed at physically connecting the university structures that align this route in the direction of the Duomo and the city centre.

Bechtler Museum
Charlotte, North Carolina, USA, 2000 (in construction)

Pland and longitudinal
section

Opposite page
View of the building

The museum is located in downtown
Charlotte, a city that has undergone rapid
urban development in recent years.
The new museum, construction of which is
planned to begin in January 2007, will house
works of art of the Bechtler family, with
important artists like Tinguely, Niki de Saint
Phalle, Picasso, Giacometti, Matisse, Miró,
Degas, Warhol, Le Corbusier and Léger.
The work plans for the construction of a
central glassed-in group of buildings with a
hall. Its play on solids and voids, guaranteed
by the presence of the glass core, will give
the construction strong plastic force. There
will be four storeys, the last of which,
illuminated from the top by numerous
skylights, juts out.
This formation ensures the special quality of
the building, which becomes the covering of
the square below.

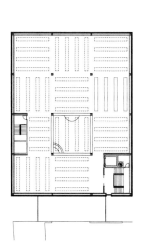
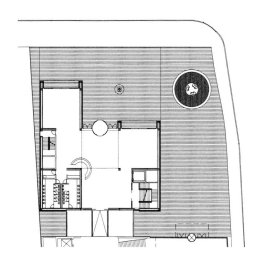
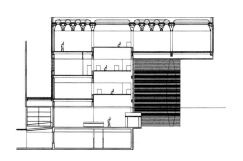

Parish of San Rocco
San Giovanni Teatino, Italy, 2006 (in construction)

Cross-section

The play on the contrast between a perimetral horizontal complex and a very plastic, highly symbolic vertical body was a choice made with the intention, on the one hand, of linking the parish services up with the fabric of the neighbourhood and on the other, with reaffirming as a *unicum* the presence of the church as a sacred space in the city. The form is monolithic, exceptional with respect to the fabric of the building, and explicitly refers to the millennial memory of ecclesiastical types whose forms emerge with respect to the fabric. In today's panorama, the new whole powerfully reaffirms the symbolic and metaphorical values as well as the functional ones, and reclaims a presence that can speak of its objectives of spirituality.

The construction of the new site is on the northwest side of the underlying structure, redefining the corner of the block between Via Cavour and Via Roma. The church, an exceptional unit rotated with respect to the entire system, was conceived of as a single volume that reaches 30 metres in height, inclined at 30 degrees with respect to the ground, reaching out towards the parvis and cut at the top only by a great opening in the form of a cross. The weekday chapel is on the side of the church; the parish centre is placed perpendicularly to Via Roma and the covered colonnade is on the other end of the parish centre. Delimited on three sides by the church, by the porticoes of the parish centre and the covered colonnade, the parvis, which becomes the place of social and religious gathering, thus the central element of the entire complex.

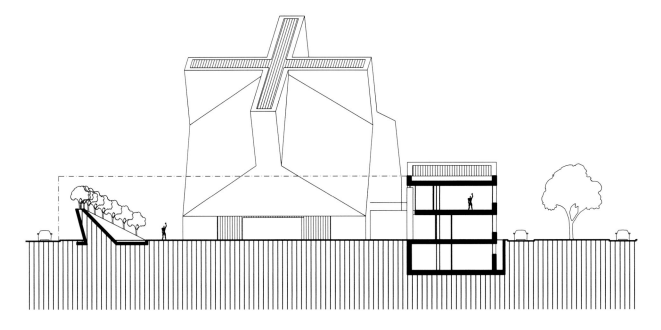

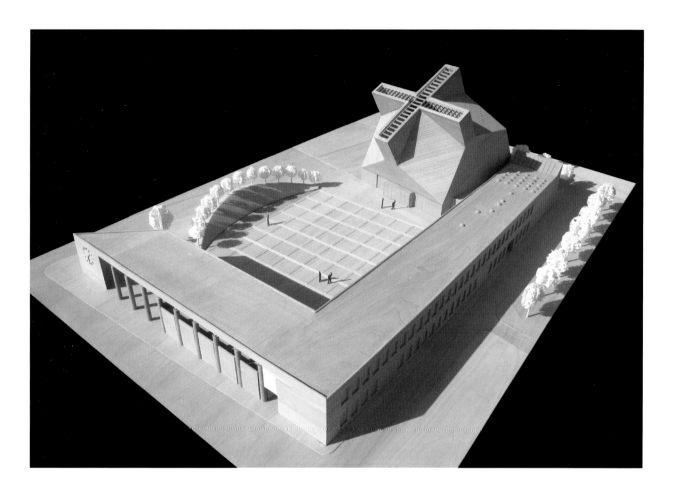

Above
Model

Below
Planimetry

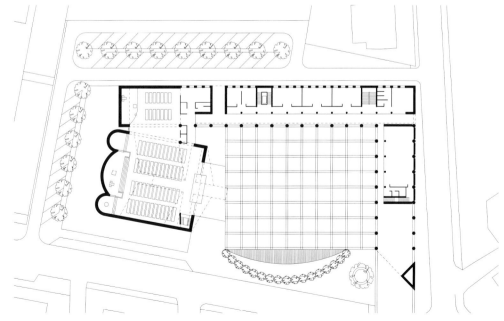

Thought

Fragments

Architecture is a Challenge

To do one's work every day, everywhere, with problems that arouse great themes and little details alike, is a way of living architecture as a trade rather than as a profession.
The trade of the architect is a filter through which to take action and dream of holding out against the contradictions of one's own time, and this filter can continuously kindle hopes. The true generator of architecture is light. Without light, there is no space. The transformation is the final goal of the architectural act. To make architecture means to modify a balance with a new balance.
I live today's contradictions: but when I create, I discover the antibodies that I have cultivated in my deepest roots. Time is a tool to read space with. The distance in time changes my approach: four or five years later I see my constructions in a different way. Architecture must wear out in the history, in the culture and in the geography of its time, and acquire different meanings – this is its wealth. Architecture is measured in duration: in the short term, it stays in the news; you need distance to appreciate it. Making architecture means transforming a condition in nature into a condition of culture. The true client of architecture is history. There is no new solution without the past.
The sacred is one of man's fundamental needs.
I always have a pencil in hand – it helps me to think. Symmetry is not an aesthetic oddity – it is a means to control light.
The architect must know everything and be capable of forgetting everything.

M. Botta, *Quasi un Diario. Frammenti intorno all'architettura*, Le Lettere, Florence 2003.

Abitare, May 2000

First of all, it is to the house as dwelling place that the maximum attention must be devoted. I say that if men truly lived as men, their houses would be temples: more than one hundred fifty years have gone by since this surprising observation of

Ruskin's, and the house is still at the centre of our concerns. The great territorial and technological transformations that have characterized the twentieth century have changed many aspects of everyday life, but they have also paradoxically reinforced some constants linked to the deepest feelings that characterize man's life-space.
How many times after life's great running through everyday life have we heard: "I'm tired, I'm going home" – where this statement lets man recognize how today, home is still his lost refuge, a space of protection, a privileged place of reflection and of memory, where it is possible to cultivate the human and psychological resources necessary to take on tomorrow. In the home, man finds serenity and peace through a domestic space that is friendly to him, that each day is the same but also different through the variations dictated by the continuous renewal of the solar cycle. Perhaps it is precisely because the space of the modern is marked by tension and uneasiness leading to the uprooting of man and his identity, which it is still possible to find in the home, anchored to a special place those antibodies that support the inhabitative values that man has a continuous need for. "To live in" is still always a way "to be" and hence also a way to find oneself again. Martin Heidegger observed that "living in a place comes before building", thus claiming the primacy of a condition of the habitat rooted in the geography, in the history and in the culture where, besides taking care of himself, man seeks his own roots and consolidates his own traditions. Of course, today the home feels the need for a new relationship between itself and its environment for the simple reason that the landscape and the territory seem to be inevitably condemned to progressive impoverishment. In this context, the house continues to represent a form of a *unicum* for each of us — something that cannot be repeated, something connoted by our individuality, which endeavours to fight the process of homologation and banalization of our surroundings. And this is so because we are more and more accomplices in a frenetic lifestyle that never stops, and the daily dwelling place remains a point of reference where we unconsciously

rediscover our past, our culture, our memory. The home today, and probably the home of tomorrow, responds to the transformations imposed by the external world with new forms of technology, with the electronic revolution, with new materials and the consequent unexpected forms and images that interact with our customs, our lifestyle, our sensibility. Mobility that cannot be stopped makes our dwelling place even more temporary, turning it into a place that will probably be less stable and secure than in the past. This will lead us to live in more than one home in the course of our lives, with different experiences in unexpected territorial contexts, far from our lands of origin. But this can only reinforce man's primordial need to have a place to live in [...].

M. Botta, *Quasi un Diario. Frammenti intorno all'architettura*, Le Lettere, Florence 2003, pp. 213-214.

Light and Gravity

In the work of architecture, light generates space: without light, space does not exist. Natural light gives body to plastic forms, it models the surface of materials, controls and balances geometric layouts/designs. The space generated by light is the soul of the architectural act. Constructed volumes flow together in the definition of the spaces that are the final goal of the architectural project. It is the void that dictates the spatial and functional relationships, that controls the visual layouts, that generates possible emotions, expectations, interpretations. Light is a natural entity that exists above and beyond the architectural act and that, in comparison with the constructed work, finds its *raison d'être* in time passing by, along the arc of the solar cycle, in the continuous sequence of the seasons. Light, for the architect, is the visible sign of a relationship that exists between the work of architecture and the cosmic values of the surroundings; it is the element that shapes the work in the specific environmental context, describing its latitude and orientation, and relating the structure to special characteristics of the environment. Gravity is the force that connects the work of architecture to the earth. One might say that is it the *raison d'être* of the building principle in search of balance to transmit loads to the ground. The first sign of building comes from placing a stone on the ground. Instead of stone, once must hence also speak of stone on the ground: all architecture carries in its breast this absolute condition of being part of the earth. Through the constructed work, man perpetuates confrontation with the earth-mother and commits an action that transforms a condition of nature into an act of culture. To place a structure on the earth is to challenge that existing equilibrium in search of new environmental values that can be witnesses of one's own time. The constructed landscape is the mirror (at times merciless) of the collectivity that it expresses. It is a way to give form to history; it is a way to give continuity to peoples who have existed – in other words, it is a way to feel oneself an arteficer of one's own time [...]. There are two fundamental aspects of the discipline – light and gravity. They are the two constants around which It is possible to undertake a reading that can highlight current interests and recent contradictions. They are realities that belong to all works of constructed architecture, so it might seem ingenuous and perhaps even useless to try to interpret their messages now. They offer a key to reading that is distant from the majority of current critics' attention. Contemporary architectural culture, through experimentation, current trends or cultural fashions, seems to move away from a comparison with these primary aspects of building (light and gravity), almost as if the architectural work could do without them. In fact, today one has the impression that operators have other concerns that are no longer directed towards the built work, but mainly at virtual aspects and comparisons, at ephemeral times, at superficial components, at playful aspects. The only ones, it seems, that still succeed in catalysing interest in debate on the subject. It might seem absurd and inappropriate to highlight aspects extraneous to these trends, above and beyond styles and languages. On the contrary, I think that calling the attention of architecture to some essential components might be a way to measure their ability to interpret the contemporary world. In the past few years' agitated proposals of extravagant experimentation and tragic annihilation, the architectural messages that emerge often escape the discipline, turning to contiguous areas – to the visual arts, to advertising or to literary interpretations, legitimating a disengagement with respect to the tasks of architecture and the search for the quality of the spaces. These attitudes are exhausted in the virtuality of theoretical debate, and leave citizens disarmed in the face of the real problems that force them to cope everyday with true urban battles, like moving around, working, parking their cars, living. It seems that the civil and social commitment that have been the foundations of the discipline for millennia have disappeared. New expressive forms yield to the laws suggested by the homologation of the "diktats" of fashion and the market, where everything – and I mean everything – is reduced to merchandise to take in and evaluate solely on the basis of economic interest. Before this disarming picture, I think I can see that there are still a few margins for coming together in creating works that can stand as positive expressions and assume the responsibility and great potential of our times. In the current environmental confusion due to rapid transformations, a firm point for possible critical resistance might be able to pass through re-reading the city as a specific space that can take on the burden of collective aspirations.

G. Cappellato (ed.), *Mario Botta. Luce e Gravità. Architetture 1993-2003*, exhibit catalogue, Editrice Compositori, Bologna 2003, pp. 8-11.

History and Memory

I am profoundly convinced that the work of the architect today opens a new dimension of research on the space of memory. It might seem paradoxical, but the more "acceleration" there is in life, the more need there is for "memory". This is because acceleration is directly proportional to oblivion. The faster we live, the more we forget. For the architect then, as compensation, the space of memory intervenes, which is not only remembrance or nostalgia, but the need for emotions, for sentiments, for what has been experienced. It is a territory sprinkled with tried and consolidated images that fill up the spaces of our childhood, places that we associate with faraway, filtered and fantastic places; places lived in by previous generations, and that we re-live in our imaginations. The construction of the space of man's life – architecture – is an element of artifice with respect to nature. It is a way to indicate the transformations enacted by man and to experience new emotions. These are values that construct our identity and the are part of our DNA. They are emotions and images of our past lives; they are the remembrance – perhaps fleeting – of metaphorical values that are at times stronger than technical and functional experiences. This is also why the transformations put into effect by architecture become fundamental parts of the human landscape. They are images that are put forward again in time with different meanings. Forms of architecture are icons which we refer to continually. Architecture speaks of the history of man; and it is always the mirror – at times merciless – of the social community. Perhaps all of this is why we are at ease in the historical centres of Italian cities. Everything speaks of a past that we easily recognize as a friend and in which we have grown up culturally. It is a landscape in which we recognize our very identity. Often we do not discover signs of contemporariness, but nonetheless we feel at ease. Perhaps this is why we unconsciously feel the need to relate to the world of extinct peoples.

Thus fascination with these places is created – because we see them with a temporal and historical distance. Perhaps contemporary architecture with its buildings is only slightly successful in supporting a feeling for life that can succeed in maintaining the sense of historicism at the same time?

Not exactly. I believe that history, as stratification, is also enriched through the contemporary sign. We appreciate the historical city precisely because we get a glimpse of a testimonial and a sign of the past, but we also discover the reasons for our own time. I do not see conflict between the new and the past. Instead, I see a dialogue, a comparison, in that the new needs the ancient in order to feel like it is part of history. However, the old needs the new to suggest a reading of the here and now. To sum everything up in a few words, one could conclude that between the old and the new, a relationship of mutual giving and taking has sprung up. Artists perform an analogous operation: Picasso made history through the re-enactment of an archaic, vegetal, erotic sign; Henry Moore uprooted the archetype of the woman-mother from time; Paul Klee interpreted the image of the child present in each of us in a contemporary way. The great creative minds go back through the great past, interpreting it and enriching it in continuation.

AA. VV., *Mario Botta, Architektur und Gedächtnis*, FSB Franz Schneider, Brakel 2005, pp. 45-53.

The Architecture of the Sacred

Architecture has all of the elements of the sacred: it brings an added value to the condition of nature, transforming it into a condition of culture that "sacralizes" the virgin soil. Moreover, from my point of view, architecture possesses other elements that belong to the sacred. The founding act, hence the moment in which a microcosm is delimited with respect to a macrocosm, the idea of characterizing the inside in a different way from the outside, the idea of threshold, the idea of limit, the idea of light … they are all parameters that flow together to give a sacred aspect to civic buildings, too: to the Museum, to the Theatre, to the Library.
In the course of my experience designing buildings, I have somewhat re-dimensioned the idea of the sacred in itself. It now seems to me as though the sacred must be of necessity linked to the context, like all architectural facts. I think that the interpretation of the place is a very important factor, which the recent construction of churches

has not duly taken into account. Sacred architecture in the twentieth century has been the territory of eccentricity, of experimentation that has often not been legitimate either with respect to history or – and above all – with respect to the context. A church must be important as an "institution" for those who do not go to church, too, because it connotes a place of union, of prayer, of silence – which the city needs. The city must also be composed of parts that do not necessarily have to be used. A square is also beautiful for those who do not go into it; a theatre is also part of the collective imagination for those who do not go to the theatre, just as the church represents the expression of collective identity for those who do not necessarily use it. My interest in the sacred in twenty years of experimentation has often been due to the fact that I have also been able to consider values not directly related to use – or functional ones – but rather to privilege the evocative aspect of architecture, that is, to go back to speaking to the primordial needs of man to make visitors feel something.
Here we are entering a space that is architecture's own. I know that in order to build a sacred space, it is first of all necessary to believe in building, hence in architecture. I do not think one can build if he does not believe in the need for sacred space. In this space, the visitor must be ready to go beyond the limits of his or her own everyday experience: light, which generates space, lends itself as a carrying element of this flight beyond function; natural materials like stone, marble, terracotta, then make spaces concrete. Nevertheless, in my churches, geometry is fundamental in order to feel like one is in a state of balance with the constructed parts, for the overall control of space. These are all elements that lead to a reflection on perfection, on beauty in order to create alternative spaces with respect to the shopping centres or garages that are typical of contemporary culture. The architecture of the sacred must be an antidote to the architecture of the ephemeral, of the consumerism of the contemporary world.

A. Coppa, interview with Mario Botta for the exhibit *Architetture del Sacro*, Florence, in *Libero*, 29 April 2005.

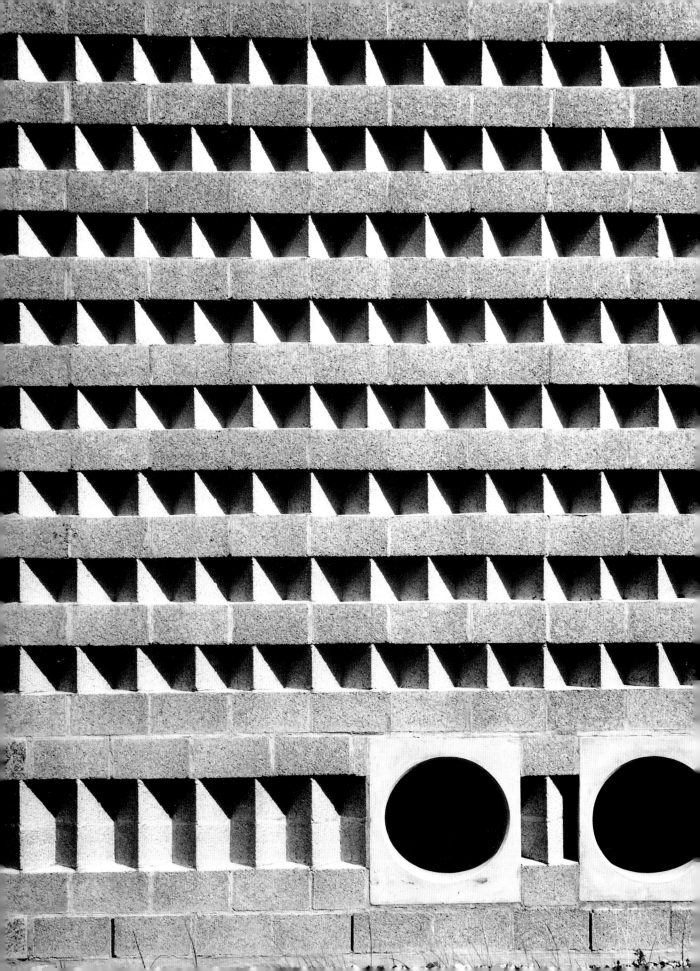

Gabriele Basilico

Round house, Stabio 1982
pp. 94-95

Mario Carrieri

Single-family home, Morbio Superiore 1984
pp. 92, 96-97

Alberto Flammer

Single-family home, Massagno 1984
p. 98

Ransila 1 Building, Lugano 1985
p. 99

Cathedral of the Resurrection, Evry 1996
pp. 100-101

Enrico Cano

Tata Consultancy Services Administrative Building (TCS),
Deccan Park, Hyderabad 2005
p. 102

Tata Consultancy Services Administrative Building (TCS),
Nuova Delhi 2002
p. 103

Pino Musi

Tent, DCC Anniversary of the Swiss Confederation,
Castelgrande, Bellinzona 1991
p. 104

Watari-um Contemporary Art Gallery, Tokyo 1990
p. 105

San Carlo, Lugano 1999
pp. 106-107

Robert Frank

Church of San Giovanni Battista, Mogno-Fusio 1995
pp. 108, 109

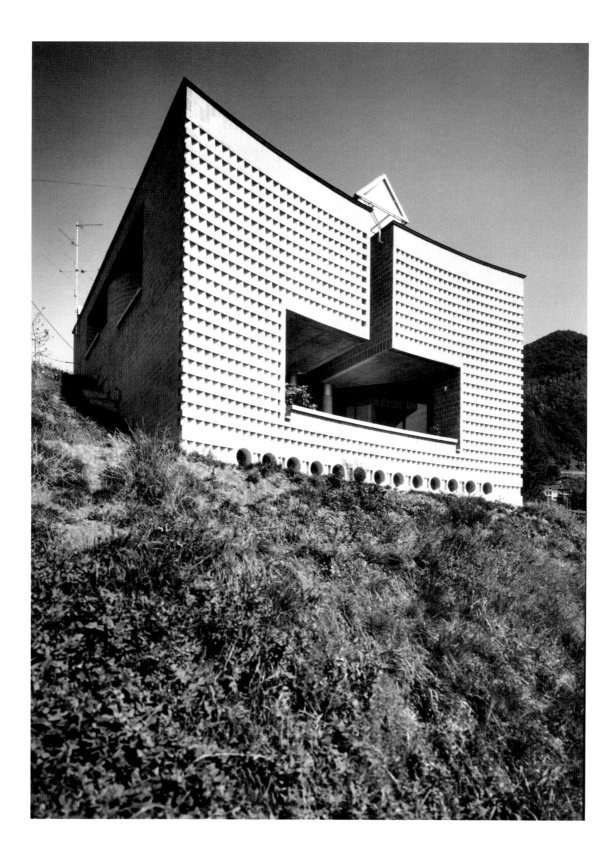

Critique

Territory, City and Geometry

Giovanni Pozzi
Architecture and Poetry

The linguistic figures that can be drawn into close relation with architectural ones are those that are based on distribution, repetition and on the exchange of the units with which the poet works. They may be symmetrical or asymmetrical positions of concepts, but are also and above all of sounds, words and linguistic segments within the obligatory space of the verse and the strophe. Rhetoric has recognized these numerous combinatory possibilities, and has classified them as alternations, chiasmi, gradations, etc. The poet, when he works in this manner, seems to be filling a void (the textual space made available by the verse or the strophe) with phonic and lexical material. It seems as though he resembles the mosaicist who spreads out his tesserae on the surface given to him. Actually, the contrary happens: the poet organizes a void: a semantic void, since the meaning of the words stored in the dictionary are not of any use to him; a phonic and rhythmic void, since the sounds and cadences of ordinary speech are meaningless to him; a graphic void, since he clears away the solids of normal typography, following instead the expressiveness of the white support.

Building by subtracting

It has often been said Botta's constructions are monolithic blocks, which have been inflicted by deep wounds in the great fissures that function as windows and skylights. Monolithic blocks, with lacerated voids caused by the subtraction of matter. I wonder if the logic that leads to that result does not take the opposite route. I wonder if the first idea, the conceptual nucleus from which Botta departs, is not instead the void; if from there and not from the solid that he starts to organize the space at this disposal. The famous question of the missing doors, of absent dividing walls (that are becoming a commonplace of the reserves or of the self-righteous derision of his architecture) would find, in this perspective, an answer that is not forced. Those walls, those doors are missing because they were never there in the first place, not because they were eliminated. The reigning void does not want to let itself be cut to bits in such a banal way. He plays master to the extent that he dictates the rules of distribution so as to leave its supreme unity intact. The house of Adam, for Botta, at least in this initial phase, was not a straw roof, or a hut made with trunks fashioned so as to form a solid, the first human nest. Rather, it was the cave ideally brought into the open air, with a film around it, a thin wrapping that preserves his image and nature: the cavern in the positive, caves wrapped in furs. The openings that make grooves in his houses are thus not wounds inflicted on the compactness of the building, but rather natural crevices, underground passages, vents emerging into the sky after this hypothetical extraction from the cavern in the earth's breast. If this is the way things are, building is, from the beginning, subtracting.

If I Had to Build a Church

Of course, if I had a church to build, I would give it to him. Mine have known it for some time, like they know that I would ask Burri and Tàpies for the figurative decoration, and (said not in jest) a Tinguely who does not think in sarcastic form of an analogue of the Cenotaph or who does not return to the slender toothed wheels of the early years, true *machines à contempler*. I said for the figurative furnishings – not for the décor – for which Botta alone would be enough. As is demonstrated by the arrangement given to our church in Lugano. There one can also grasp, despite the limited nature of the intervention, the thought that seems to guide him on the way to the sacred.
He emptied out the little church in Lugano of all of the superstructures that had accumulated on it and he whitened it with the purest – almost blinding – of whites. There he left very dark antique pieces of furniture: and he added black fixtures that support the paintings of the old abolished altars. He designed the altar, the lectern and the high-backed chairs for the celebrants; the

altar moved to the left *in cornu epistulae*, the lectern to the right *in cornu evangelii*. He left only one single line in white corresponding to the altar: in front of the lectern, the emptiness of a light grey granite floor. Let us now read in the text put before us. The colours lead to a very simple play on black and white. They are two non-chromatic colours that lead us to see an opposition of light and shadow. Why then does black not evoke that vision of the shadows that is the highest degree of the theological and mystical knowledge of God? And the white that blinding in light that is its correlative, while also being its contrary? The dialectic between voids and solids is analogous. According to earthly reasoning, the body of the whites should be found in correspondence to the lectern, in order to create a reader-listener relationship. However, Botta seems to reason with non-earthly logic. Substituting the void, he comes to tell us with the psalmist that the divine word does not stop at the ears of those present at the rite, but is spread in all of the spaces of creation (after all, the church is the symbol of the cosmos) and thus does not have elect listeners before it. Instead ,the participation of the fixed human presence in the pews is directed towards the altar, to the real Eucharistic presence *ivi transeunte e manente* in the tabernacle (thus also located to the right). The auditory relationships take place in the void; the visual ones in the solids.

Here, too, the guiding concept is apparent asymmetry that creates symmetry, of emerging uneasiness that is lulled in the stillness. Just like Christian contemplation when it is at its height. Nevertheless, this is only simple restoration. The designing of a church all his own would take Botta — as one might believe — much further, perhaps to the symbolic thresholds of the catacombs, or even to those of the open sepulchre of the Risen Christ. But how can I, dull and incompetent as I am, dare to launch hypotheses for an imagination and technical wisdom that, as the exhibit teaches, run tireless from one surprise to another?

G. Pozzi, "Quattro istantanee per Botta", in *Sull'orlo del visibile parlare*, Adelphi, Milan 1993, pp. 430-433.

Jacques Gubler
Bibliographical Zigzag

Mario Botta with Achille Castiglioni

It is a well-known fact that Botta loves to talk about his career in order to acclaim his masters, Scarpa, Le Corbusier and Kahn, thus acknowledging affiliation. Even the possibility of commenting on this affiliation with modern tradition has become one of the critical themes of his work. That happened around 1980, at the time of the revival of the Venice Biennale, with the "international exhibit of architecture". Ironically enough, Botta refused to take part in it. The Venetian slogan, the presence of the past, was so wide-ranging as to cover and to oppose partisans and adversaries of the post-modern. Almost all of the leading figures of the exhibit, both present and outgoing, wrote on Botta, either to incorporate him in the autobiographical exhibit on the post-modern condition, or to cite him as a counter-example of the prolongation of the modern dialectic. Already in 1975 at the Zurich Polytechnic, the programme of "different repetition" and the need to *weiterbauen* was simplified through "new architecture in Ticino". We repeat that Botta's presence in this debate came from his ability to copy his masters in order to reach unpredictable results, citing sources without narcissism. Botta also wrote to valorise the work of colleagues

Mario Botta with Giovanni Pozzi

and this mission is manifest in the labyrinthine title of the book, *L'arcaicità del nuovo* (The Archaicism of the New). Here, architecture makes visible "the force of totemic, fixed, hieratic figures".
[…]. The discussion on totems comes up again in the *Conversation* with Dal Co of 1989. In front of the house in Breganzona, Dal Co wondered if the poetics of emphasis and dramatics present in the assembly of elements had not in the end reached the "bizarre". He also wondered if an excess of constructive virtuosity might not lead towards "mannerism", if there weren't any added tricks. Botta responded to this provocation by saying that there was no reason to be amazed that art is provocative, that everything has been that way for years, that the "totem" in architecture corresponds to "archaic values" established by modern painting (Picasso, Klee). The architect no longer has a belly or a cave to offer. When the critic speaks of incoherence, the artist speaks of autobiographical foundations. Where the public sees Mickey Mouse's ears, the author speaks of the belvedere on pilasters and confesses: "This figure of a double skylight like frog's eyes, takes me back at least ten years". The architect explains that this new image must be understood as logical alternative to the skylight as a form of pediment (as in the cubic house in Pregassona of 1979-1980, or in the round house in Stabio of 1980-1982).

J. Gubler, Cantieri, in E. Pizzi, Mario Botta. *Opere complete*, 1985-1990, 2, Federico Motta Editore, Milan 1994, p. 6-7.

Benedikt Loderer
A Roman of Modern Forms

Botta is archaic. He has certainly learned from the moderns – Le Corbusier and Kahn were his masters – but the more distinctly he formed his vocabulary, the more he became archaic. His constructions have mass and history, the are all older than their years. They are obviously contemporary constructions, nevertheless, in them, variously transformed, there is a Mediterranean tradition that finds an echo in us

considered important in comparison with his own work. It was not a question of making the teachings of the great masters current, but of informing oneself on parallel research, which can especially be seen in the work of Siza, Ando, Galfetti and Stirling. By linking up with the work of the other, the artist planned his own *modus operandi* with a mirror-like effect. For example, the fine book on the New State Gallery by Stirling and Wilford in Stuttgart can be read as a summary of Botta's poetics. Written in 1985, the text seems to be edited specifically as a preface to this second volume of the *Complete Works*. It starts with an ironic rejection of the -isms of architecture, empty attempts at beatification. It bids adieu to the most contested –ism of the time, post-modernism, a "big circus" and "architecture that confused styles with history". Then the trilogy "work-play-gravity" was established. For Botta and Stirling, work meant that the pertinence of the idea existed only in the effort of construction and in "the test of the construction site".
[…] Botta blazes the trail: "James Stirling works. […] James Stirling has a good time. [...] James Stirling is renewed". The renewal takes place in archaicism

and arouses feelings of security, power, protection, order and attachment to one's roots. With modern forms, Botta succeeds in building *alla romana*.

Botta lasts forever. The archaic comes from remote times and will survive because Botta has never accepted anticipation; it is destined to wear away. What he builds must remain, and it must remain as he built it. His constructions are thoroughly meditated upon. They are always massive, solid, stable bodies that remain unchanged *in saecula saeculorum*. Botta is massive. He, too, must submit to the laws of physics and to the imperative of isolation. He, too, must build his walls in various strata. In the end, he, too, must adopt a tenuous external facing that is called façade. Nonetheless, his walls transmit the idea of mass and they always appear to us as heavy and powerful. They always seem to be unassailable: they are Roman walls formed of today's strata.

B. Loderer, "Romano dalle forme moderne", in E. Pizzi, *Mario Botta. Opere complete*, 1990-1997, 3, Federico Motta Editore, Milan 1998, p. 6.

Rudolf Arnheim
The Church of San Giovanni Battista in Mogno

All works of art that deserve this name are symbolic and works of architecture are no exception. [...]. Symbolic meaning is not simply an attribute to add to the building on the part of a "thinker from the outside", as a sort of adjunct interpretation, but rather is the essence and nature of architectural design itself. [...] Nevertheless, it is useful to distinguish "open" symbols from "closed" symbols. "Open" symbols are created by designers every time that they work in their field of investigation. In every culture, the solutions found tend to be standardized, replacing individual invention and thus becoming reduced to simple archetypes. [...]

In 1986, the seventeenth century church of the village was destroyed by an avalanche. In designing a new church, Botta avoided the paralysing effects of the "closed" symbols of traditional ecclesiastical architecture. His church is conceived in a modern language that is considerably different from the models of the past, but without seeking sensational novelty in any way. On the contrary, it aspires to satisfy the basic necessities of a temple for worship, simply and directly deriving the expressive characteristics of pure geometrical forms from them.

Botta's church opens towards the sky and thus satisfies Leon Battista Alberti's requirement of "being isolated and elevated above the everyday life around it". It is a simple cylinder of stone, different from the form that the inhabitants of the village were accustomed to. It is not that simple forms are extraneous to rural life[...] but having to face such a cylinder as a parish church must be surprising.

More precisely, the cylinder presents a horizontal elliptical section, and slightly above the height of a man, it is cut by an inclined plane. [...] the oblique surface of the roof makes the upper part of the cylinder acute, transforming it into a sort of bell tower standing out against the sky, like those of traditional churches. At the same time, the inclined, glass surface of the roof reaches towards the sky like the hands joined in prayer of one of the faithful, orienting the building and its relation: with the sun, as is traditional in church construction — without forgetting that the architect gave the inclined surface of the roof the perfect form of a circle. The inner perimeter, at floor level with a rectangular base, forces the walls to gradually adapt as they rise to the circular roof, in a continuous transformation course upon course. This sophisticated change is not easy to visualize, since the main axis of the elliptical cylinder of the building is oriented on a right angle with respect to the median line of the roof.

After the complexity of the form is understood, the spirit of the assembly of the faithful is placed in relation to the sublimation of the space of earthly life and projected towards the perfection of the circular *oculus* of the roof. But since the roof is inclined, the faithful are allowed to see it only in perspective. In fact, the frontal, complete view is

reserved solely for the place where the crucifix is located, on the wall above the apse. Here, the position of the figure of Christ coincides with the perpendicularity of the circle of the roof.
In this way, the entire form simultaneously crystallizes the symbolic interrelation evoked between the ellipse and the circle. [...]. With the development of Mannerism, architecture with an elliptical plan was introduced. Panofsky cited Michelangelo's first project for the Tomb of Julius II as one of the first examples. During the seventeenth century, the ellipse came to be a commonly used form. In fact, in the church of San Carlo alle Quattro Fontane in Rome, Borromini used the main axis of the church, positioning the entrance from one side and the apse from the other. In his church in Mogno, Botta used [...] the smaller diameter of the ellipse as the main axis of the building, which at the same time became harmonized with the dominant axis of symmetry of the roof. Its composition is a modern synthesis of the traditional juxtaposition between the circle and the ellipse, thus drawing two forms into a conflicting relation. From the philosophical and theological point of view, it is a parallel between the controlled, square space of the "terrestrial" ellipse and the circular roof of the "sacred kingdom".
It is clear that when architectural constructions go beyond "closed" symbols associated with their conventional function, and instead suggest "open" symbols, their meaning will be expressed by sensitivity to the human attitude rather than to mere practical application. In the case of the religious architecture in question, it means that the designer started with the most profound human qualities to arrive at religious ritual: in the case of Mogno, Catholicism. The architect could be Catholic, visualizing the human qualities which the artist is up against through doctrine, or he could also be of a different religion, or he could be an atheist.

R. Arnheim, "Notes on religious architecture", in *Languages of Design*, 1993, 3, pp. 247-251 (It. transl., "Note a proposito dell'architettura religiosa", in *Domus*, 757, 1994, pp. 82-85).

Lionello Puppi
Space, Geometry and Light

A profound vocation and ancient integrity lie at the base of Mario Botta's practice of the trade of architect. An itinerary amidst the works that have dotted Botta's career will allow us to discover some of the constants that characterize the work of this architect from Ticino – work undertaken, in fact, "as a vocation", without the possibility of dodging that obligatory passage of suffering, which finds peace only when "everyday anxiety is appeased on the white paper of the drawing board". And that is also why Palladio identified one of the "prohibited" characteristics in the figure of the architect as the fact that he is born "not only for himself but to be of use to others". Mario Botta resolves this problem with the formula "the true question of architecture is never aesthetic, but ethical".
"The values that man has within him are also the values that architecture must bear witness to" notes Botta, charging the architect with the task of concretely translating that world of meanings that man constructs by abstraction. These are the fundamental springboards of spatial language that – letting geometry, light and silence speak – give us absolute events of the purest architectural poetry.

L. Puppi, "Lo spazio, la geometria e la luce", in *Mario Botta. Luce e Gravità, architetture 1993-2003*, ed. G. Cappellato, exhibit catalogue, Editrice Compositori, Bologna 2003, p. 27.

Heinrich Thelen
The Drawings of Mario Botta

For Mario Botta, drawing is one of the essential vital functions, comparable to breathing. It is difficult to run into the architect without his inseparable "toccalapis" in hand, which he uses not only to draw, but also simply to attract attention of the interlocutor on the point under discussion. For Mario Botta, drawing is also a moment to check his architectural ideas by fixing them graphically, or better, the moments, the phases, the "hinges" of the creative process.

Therefore, for the architect, drawings are moments in a broader designing *iter*; they are an instrument for approximation, not works of art in themselves – drawings traced out with a straight, energetic line, free hand, on "his" parchment paper. Among Botta's very few tools, a metal ruler in millimetres, not much higher than a roll of paper. The passage from model for the project developed with graphic means to model created by means of printed graphics takes place in the tower in Lugano, where the sketches that, by the way, are also beautiful – a joy for the eyes – become reality.

H. Thelen, "I disegni di Mario Botta", in *Mario Botta. Luce e Gravità*, 1993-2003, exhibit catalogue, Editrice Compositori, Bologna 2003, p. 35.

Fulvio Irace
Santa Maria degli Angeli, Monte Tamaro

In the mountain air of Alpe Foppa, Mario's gestures become calm and relaxed, while he slowly walks down the porphyry walkway that goes from the mountain to the audacious end of the belvedere, open like an eye out onto the panorama ranging from the lake of Lugano, through Monte Ceneri and Bellinzona, all the way to Lago Maggiore. It can be reached only from Rivera, a few kilometres from Lugano, by a cable car that slowly goes up the 1500 vertical metres necessary to reach the powerful viaduct that actually culminates in the terraced roof of a circular chapel, from which it symmetrically descends to regain, on the ground, access to the interior.

Appropriately named after Our Lady of the Angels (Santa Maria degli Angeli), the final effort of the architect, assisted on the occasion by a rare partner, Enzo Cucchi, an artist from the Marches, appear from afar as a metaphysical bridge, dizzyingly detaching itself from the ground to then launch itself apparently in infinite suspension into the void below. Singular in formal conception, this secluded sacred building – which possesses something of the place of devotion and at the same time family memorial – is the fortunate result of an

extraordinary story, for the way it was commissioned, for the special quality of its location, for the course of the definition of its design. Stretched out like a powerful bulwark halfway up imposing Monte Tamaro, the chapel in fact was born of a dream and a desire: dedicated to the memory of a dear departed person, Santa Maria degli Angeli is a private act of faith on the part of an entrepreneur, Egidio Cattaneo, who in this way wanted to celebrate his faith in architecture's ability to become human substance and not simply

Mario Botta with Enzo Cucchi

117

representation of itself. In identifying, on his part, the essence of religion dictated with the intrinsically religious nature of his work, Botta interpreted the commission as the act of giving a gift: with accentuation – that is, symbolic and emotional, transferred from the architectural object to the structure of the place. Like all acts of devotion, the chapel makes clear its nature as an offering and at the same time its connotation of commitment directly springing from inner conviction. "The religious value of a work of art and its artistic value", Botta maintains, "spirituality is not a clerical prerogative [...] whoever enters this space will find his God".

Architecture, which identifies place, thus encounters art, which individualizes architecture, and both contribute to constructing an intrinsic coherence, supported by the desire of the receiver and by the knowledge of the iconologist Giovanni Pozzi, who "wrote" for Botta the script for the entire decorative cycle dedicated to the cult of Mary.

The result is not only a non-conventional tribute to the ideal of a modern *Gesamtkunstwerk*, but more importantly a demonstration of the impressive power of fusion of art and architecture in a challenging, measureless environmental situation and in an epoch-making context incapable of credible certainties. In this period of history, barren of hope but pregnant with obscure delusions and frustrating expectancy, the re-emergence of the mystic seems in fact to confirm Mircea Eliade's exhortation to recognize the mystery of the sacred camouflaged in the profane. Challenged on the validity of its foundations, the entire model of contemporary civilization is creaking, and shows signs of excessive wear and tear, especially when it comes to giving concrete answers to the widespread, collective aspiration to new forms of religiosity. At the point where old and new clash, they thus end up with the accumulation of questions and tensions that lay bare the incapacity of laymen and the clergy to understand each other, as well as their mutual impotence in giving answers that are not simplistic or anachronistic shortcuts

repudiating some tradition of thought or another. It is not a matter of chance that a sore spot *par excellence* of this obvious lack of connection is still – and not since today – the entire area of artistic and architectural research, where the process of progressive laicisation promoted by avant-garde movements is identified *tout court* with the emancipation of "content" and with the "abstraction" of forms. This ideological vision of modernity that mistrusts any manifestation of mysticism found, in the 1950s, its clearest expression in Giulio Carlo Argan's protest against the "irrationality" of Le Corbusier's famous chapel in Ronchamp: "Modern architecture, whose tradition is secular – charged Argan – can build churches, without, however, contradicting or diminishing itself. The error begins when, in order to build churches, one pretends to invent a style ad hoc – the style of modern sacred architecture. Modern architecture, which has a civil and profane origin, has created, on the social themes of habitation and work, forms that can pass without causing any scandal in religious architecture [...]religion takes on the form of social life [...] the church is a place of meeting, not a means to exhort and incite to ecstasy".

Therefore, today it is precisely this reduction of the mystery of the sacred to the mere mechanics of co-existence with the civil that shows clear signs of insufficiency, and as a consequence, brings out the inadequacy of an undifferentiated approach to the project that considers the theme of religious architecture as a simple absolution of any sort of social function. In this sense, the project of the church experiences the aporia of contemporary architecture and, and as the architect Augusto Romano Burelli notes, "the conflict is glaring because it comes about between the strong theological statute of the church and the weak statute of the architecture that should invent it".

F. Irace, in *Il Sole 24 Ore*, 16/10/1994, now in F. Irace, "Dimenticare Vitruvio", *Il Sole 24 Ore*, Milano 2001, pp. 177-180.

Bibliography

M. Botta, *Quasi un diario. Frammenti intorno all'architettura, Le Lettere*, Florence 2003.

M. Botta, *La cantina di Suvereto*, La Quadra Editrice, Brescia 2003.

F. Dal Co (ed.), *Mario Botta. Architettura 1960-1985*, Electa, Milan 1985.

E. Pizzi (ed.), *Mario Botta Opere complete*, voll.1, 2, 3, Federico Motta Editore, Milan 1993,1994, 1998.

F. Irace, U. Perucchi-Petri, G. Pozzi, Mario Botta, Enzo Cucchi, *La cappella del Monte Tamaro*, Umberto Allemandi & C. Editore, Turin 1994.

I. Sakellaridou, *Mario Botta. Poetica dell'architettura*, RCS Libri, Milan 2000 (repr. Rizzoli / Skira, Milan 2002).

G. Cappellato (ed.), *Mario Botta. Luce e Gravità, architetture 1993-2003*, exhibit catalogue, Editrice Compositori, Bologna 2003.

AA. VV., *Mario Botta. Il Museo di Arte Moderna e Contemporanea di Trento e Rovereto*, Skira, Milan 2003.

AA. VV., *Mario Botta. Chiesa a Seriate*, Skira, Milan 2004.

AA.VV., *Mario Botta, Architektur und Gedächtnis*, FSB Franz Schneider, Brakel 2005.

G. Cappellato (ed.), *M. Botta, Architetture del Sacro. Preghiere di Pietra*, exhibit catalogue, Editrice Compositori, Bologna 2005.

Other texts in the anthological sections:

G. Pozzi, "Quattro istantanee per Botta", in *Sull'orlo del visibile parlare*, Adelphi, Milano 1993, pp. 430-431, 432-433.

R. Arnheim, Notes on religious architecture, in *Languages of Design*, 1993, 3, pp. 247-251 (trad. it. in Note a proposito dell'architettura religiosa / Notes on religious architecture, in *Domus*, 757, 1994, pp. 82-85).

F. Irace, in *Il Sole 24 Ore*, 16/10/1994 (now in F. Irace, *Dimenticare Vitruvio, Il Sole 24 Ore*, Milan 2001, pp. 177-180).

A. Coppa, interview with Mario Botta, *Architetture del Sacro, Firenze*, in *Libero*, 29/04/2005.

Photographic references

Archivio Botta, Lugano: 85, 113, 114
Gabriele Basilico, Milan: 94, 95
Robert Canfield, San Rafael: 48 top
Enrico Cano, Como: cover, 6, 12-13, 16-17, 18, 32,
38, 39 top, 54-55, 56-57, 57 top, 57 bottom, 58, 60
top, 60 bottom, 61, 71, 72, 72-73, 76, 80, 102, 103
Mario Carrieri, Milan: 92, 96, 97
Andrea Cometta, Pedrinate: 117
Marco D'Anna, Lugano: 26 top, 27, 35, 37, 110
Alberto Flammer, Losone: 98, 99, 100, 101
Foto Paritani di Pari Roberto e Tani Sergio, Rimini: 26
Robert Frank, Mabou Cape Breton, Nova Scotia:
108, 109
Pino Musi, Milan: rear cover, 8-9, 10-11, 28, 36, 40,
41, 43, 45 top, 45 bottom, 47, 49, 66, 67, 68 top,
68 bottom, 69, 104, 105, 106, 107
Ralph Richter, Düsseldorf: 64, 65
Paolo Rosselli, Milan: 86
Pietro Savorelli, Bagno a Ripoli (FI): 14-15
STUDIO DIM ASSOCIATI, Florence: 78, 83
Cornelia Suhan, Dortmund: 63
Young Chea Park, Seoul: 50, 52, 53

For all pictures and sketches, unless otherwise
indicated, Studio Architetto Botta

The publisher is available for any queries regarding
pictures that have not been accredited